"Weapons!"   —F

"It's hard to accurately convey the Jacob have made on the Wild organization. In one short visit, they erased years of progress and left a hole we are still trying to climb out of. Strangely, we still love the boys and wish them the best (just not here in the State of Hockey)."   **—Matt Majka, President, Minnesota Wild**

"The Kings were one of the first teams to reach out to the boys. We thought we saw something unique and intriguing, and assuming they had talent, we felt our players could pick up a few tips. Sadly, that was a mistake. But our players did enjoy showing the boys how to take a hit!"

**—Michael Altieri, Sr. Vice President, Marketing,
Communications, and Content, LA Kings**

"Being the #1 Draft Pick this year was awesome—but getting pointers from Olly and Jacob was even cooler. . . . hope their coaching doesn't get me kicked out of the league!"

—Jack Hughes, #1 NHL Draft Pick 2019, New Jersey Devils

"These quirky characters crashed our 75/25 Anniversary Legends Gala held at historic Maple Leaf Gardens in Toronto. Apparently, they consider themselves 'legends,' but we had never heard of them. After a short ruckus, the

Canadian Mounties (on hand to guard the Stanley Cup) escorted them out of the building."

—Jeff Denomme, President and
CEO, Hockey Hall of Fame

"I was able to teach these rookies a few tricks, but they're still a long way from a career in the NHL—in fact I'm not sure I'd even let them off the bench, but I applaud their passion."

—Jeremy "J.R." Roenick, 20 year NHL season career veteran, NBC and NHL Network Sports Analyst, Author

"Olly and Jacob keep hounding me and Petey [Elias Pettersson] to do a 2v2 chally, but we all know that will just end up in embarrassment for the boys."

—Brock Boeser, Vancouver Canucks

"I thought I knew a lot about hockey until I met the boys in Airdrie last summer. They told me I didn't know how to coach. It turns out they were right. I wasn't paying enough attention to the fundies."

—Pavel Barber, Stickhandling Specialist

"Didn't know what to expect when I first met these two wagons. But glad I did, Jacob taught me a new way to score from the blue, I don't know what Olly did . . ."

—Matt Dumba, Minnesota Wild

"Two future Hall of Famers."

—Elias Pettersson, Vancouver Canucks

"Twenty-five years covering hockey, I'm not sure I've covered two bigger locker-room misfits. But they [give] pretty good quotes and are kinda funny, so I've learned to tolerate them."

—Michael Russo, *The Athletic*

"They do a yeoman's job teaching the fundies!"

—Tom Reid, Retired NHL Defenceman and Sports Broadcaster

"Those boys don't know jack about professional hockey —but it was sure fun showing them how to check!"

—Kyle Clifford, LA Kings

"As a premiere performance hockey brand, CCM prides itself on its R&D team with some of the best players in the world—McDavid, Crosby, Ovechkin, Price. Olly and Jacob are definitely not on our R&D team, and we'd rather they not use our stuff, even if they aren't making it off the bench. It's just not a good look."

—Rick Blackshaw, CEO, CCM Hockey

"The kids that attend our tournaments love the boys, so we brought them in to have some fun. Unfortunately our liability insurance rates doubled, but our hockey IQ tripled. Good trade-off.

—Kevin Mann, President and CEO, 200x85 LLC (CCM World Invites)

OLLY POSTANIN AND JACOB ARDOWN

THE FUNDIES

THE ESSENTIAL HOCKEY GUIDE FROM ON THE BENCH

PENGUIN

an imprint of Penguin Canada, a division of Penguin Random House Canada Limited

Canada • USA • UK • Ireland • Australia • New Zealand • India • South Africa • China

First published 2019

www.penguinrandomhouse.ca

LIBRARY AND ARCHIVES CANADA CATALOGUING IN PUBLICATION

Title: The fundies : the essential hockey guide from On the bench / Olly Postanin and Jacob Ardown.
Names: Postanin, Olly, author. | Ardown, Jacob, author.
Identifiers: Canadiana (print) 20190101415 | Canadiana (ebook) 20190101431 | ISBN 9780735236981 (softcover) | ISBN 9780735236998 (HTML)
Subjects: LCSH: Hockey–Humor.
Classification: LCC GV847 .P67 2019 | DDC 796.962.02/07–dc23

Book and cover design: Andrew Roberts
Cover image: Jenelle Andersen
Upper Deck card images used with permission from The Upper Deck Company. All rights reserved.
Tape Job images curtesy of DaleAnn Murphy and Barb Nelson
Image of Brock Boeser provided by Murphy Management
Image of Teddy Purcell used with permission from Spittin' Chiclets
All other photos courtesy of the authors

Edited by DaleAnn Murphy

Printed and bound in Canada

10 9 8 7 6 5 4 3 2 1

Penguin
Random House
PENGUIN CANADA

To the fans who love the game as much as we do

—thanks for following the fundies.

OTB PLEDGE

I pledge allegiance to the puck.
May my ankles be sturdy,
my dangles be dirty,
and always respect the flow.

DISCLAIMER

It's our mission to teach people everywhere the fundies, but while we can show you how it's meant to be done, no one should attempt to play the game like we do, because no one else could ever possibly be that good. So, when playing hockey, or any sport, safety is the top priority. Take each and every precaution required or recommended.

www.onthebench.life
Inquiries: management@onthebench.life

OTB CHANNELS
YouTube: On the Bench
facebook.com/officialonthebench
instagram.com/on.the.bench
twitter.com/onthebenchcrew
Snapchat: thebenchcrew
twitch.tv/onthebenchcrew

CONTENTS

GLOSSARY

A quick breakdown of all the need-to-know terms before you can learn the fundies. There's a lot of ground to cover, so you'll need to keep up.

Apple - assisted goal, an assist

B-way - breakaway
Backy - backhand
Bender - bad player
Bennys - benefits
Bisccy - the biscuit is the puck, of course
Booger bag - nose, or face
Bucket, bucky - helmet
Burnin' (hoof) - skating quickly

C-check - cross-check
Cappy - the captain, boys
Celly - celebration
Chally - challenge
Cheese - shot
Chel - NHL, or NHL video game
Chicken wings - arms
Chin curtains - beards

Clappy, clappies, clappers - slapshot
Compy - composite stick
Conny - contract
Crossies - crossovers
Crucie - crucial

Dimpies - golf balls
Dome - head
Duster - same as a bender

Elbies - elbow pads
Eppie - episode (as in OTB video episode of the fundies)

Face massagers - fists
Fifth line - officials, refs, and linesmen
Finger pillows - gloves
Flow - hair, or mop top (all beauties have good flow)
Folded fives - punches

Fundies - fundamentals

Grease your snapper - shoot the puck
Greasy - style of play
Grocery stick - useless player

Hippie – hip check

Ice piggy – referee

Jiblets – teeth

Lettuce – hair
Lip sweater – mustache

Melon – your noggin (head)
Missy – a hard shot, but not in the net
Mop – same as your lettuce, or hair

Numbies – hockey number

One-tee – one timer shot

Pigeon – winger, forward
Praccy – practice (gotta do it, boys)
Pylon – slow skater, or duster

Rip rope – score a goal
Richie – ritual
Rock pile – a pylon, boys
Rockets – babes, hot girls

Seasy – season (also SZN)

Scouties – hockey scouts
Setty – set-up
Shorty – short-handed goal
Shouldy, shouldies – shoulder pads
Sin bin – penalty box
Snappie – snapshot
Snizzy (or snizz) – a goal
Spenny – suspension
Stripes – same as ice piggy
Stutty step – stutter step
Suey – suicide pass

Targgy – target
Teamies – teammates
Tendy – the brick house in the net, goal tender, goalie
Tilly – a tilt, or fight
Timby – the wood or timber, hockey stick
T.J. – tape job on your stick
Top corns – top corner of the net (where Olly and Jacob shoot)
Twig – timby, or the stick you use to send bisccies to the tendy
Twine – hockey net

Warmies – warm-ups

Wheel - flirt (as in wheelin' the rockets)

Wheels - skates, how fast you skate

Wrappy - Wrap-around goal

Wristy - wrist shot

Zebra - referee or linesman

INTRODUCTION

Hey boys, welcome to the first-ever **written** eppie. If you're reading this book, you probably already know Olly and Jacob, but in case you missed a few details about our greasy hockey careers and how we started, let's get you up to speed.

First, what are the fundies? Plain and simple, fundies are the fundamentals. The basics of everything and anything hockey. You didn't even know you needed the fundies until we broke the Internet and introduced them to you. With the game getting softer every year, our presence is needed more than anyone knows. If you want to be the best, you need to always move forward. We aren't just reckless with our bodies—we feel no pain because there isn't any room for pain in the fundies. That is why we are here: to teach you how hockey is supposed to be played.

A lot of people like to ask, "Why aren't you in the league if you're so good?" And we like to respond with something like, "Are you going to ask stupid questions all day?" It's easy to see that we are far better than any player to enter the game. Each generation has a player that is unquestionably talented, such as Al MacInnis, the great lip sweater that is Lanny McDonald, and today's stars like Brock Boeser and Connor McDavid. They still don't have anything on us, though. Don't believe us? Why are they all asking to be in an eppie and learn the fundies from us? Without a doubt, our advice and training could bring players like Lanny out of retirement and make him even more successful than he was before. (Still waiting for that call, Lanny.)

We don't play in the show because it isn't at the level it needs to be for us to have any sort of challenge. That is why we are training the entire NHL, one eppie at a time—to create some competition that would make it worth our while to play. So, yeah, we are the best, and you need the fundies!

1 WHO WE ARE

OLLY POSTANIN RW • BANGLADESH TIGERS

Play-maker • Goal-scorer • Complete package • Former MVP •
Record holder for least amount of time played in one season

Olly Postanin is the name, boys. I started my life in Newmarket, Ontario. I guess you can say that is where a legend was made. My journey began like any other kid growing up in Canada—rippin' rope at a young age. My formative years were spent playing hockey in Elliot Lake, learning to wheel on the mini skating rink my dad built on the deck in our backyard.

I spent countless hours perfecting my craft—shooting, skating, fighting, and . . . sitting on the bench. That's right, boys, my dad benched me. A lot. I'm still not sure why. Maybe it was because I was dummying my older brother all day on the rink while he pretended he was Wayne Gretzky. Naturally, I took liberties on him with a lot of slashies, a few hits from behind, you know—normal brother stuff.

OLLY POSTANIN

HOCKEY

It was also during this time that I scooped my first pair of cowboy boots. A lot of people ask me why I wear the boots, and it's pretty simple: they are the best footwear for running because they are so aerodynamic. They're built for speed, which makes me pretty much unstoppable.

When it was time to start playing organized hockey at the age of four, I was already an absolute weapon. Not only was I the only player in Timbits Hockey that could raise the puck and go top corns on the tendy (making him look like a complete pylon), I was also the only four-year-old kid to get spenny'd for fighting. You may be thinking, "Who fights in Timbits Hockey?" Well, the kid I dropped the mitts with was chirping me for wearing a Jofa bucket. He taunted me with "That's a dad helmet," so naturally I did what any beauty would do—I dropped my finger pillows and tossed a few hammers at his dome. I lost that fight but learned an important lesson: hitting the scoresheet was the most important part in hockey—besides the flow, obviously.

Because of my prowess on the ice, I was scouted at an early age for the Bangladesh Pro League.

It was a hard decision to make: stay and play minor-league hockey or crush it overseas. So, like any smart ten-year-old would do, I packed my duffle and all my mini sticks and hit the road (and the sea—Bangladesh is a trek).

After seven seasons playing pro in Bangladesh, I proudly led the league in PIMs and least amount of ice time played. You're probably wondering how I lasted so long and accomplished so much in the league. Keep reading and you'll learn some important secrets that led to my record-setting career.

Fastest wheels seen on ice • Well-rounded legend with mastery in all vital hockey skills • Set and broke every record imaginable, including most games as a healthy scratch

I have played puck for as long as I can remember, setting unbreakable records, easily marking me a legend. On top of that, I am also likely the humblest player in the game. Even if it seems like I'm cocky, I'm not. I just know how great I am. There's a big difference. I have been called the purest of beauties. It should be easy to see why, but if you weren't able to pick it up, I'll break it down for you.

First thing to point out is the style, boys. Rockin' the deadly lettuce on my dome, blazin' in the wind while I burn hoof. And, of course, the nasty beard. Facial hair is super crucial to your game-play, boys; that's why I chose to go with the "handle chops." My favourite colour is plaid, so naturally it's the only vest I wear. And the Velcro wheels are built for speed.

THE UPPER DECK COMPANY

GOODWIN CHAMPIONS

JACOB ARDOWN

HOCKEY

As for the game-play, boys, I'm not sure where to start. I made it to the Virgin Islands Elite Hockey League because I'm such a well-rounded player. I tore up the league with the Virgin Islands Coconut Cutters for seven years. I was initially brought in because of my greasy snapper, but the league had no idea what they were getting when I signed my big conny.

Early in my career with the Coconut Cutters, I set a record that still has not been beat and likely never will be: most stick infractions in one period, boys. I set it high, racking up 13 infractions in the first period before the coach kicked me out of the game. I hadn't been scoring much at the time, trying to get into the routine of my new team. So, like any natural athlete, I found a way to flood the scoresheet.

Some people have called me a "goal-scorer's goal-scorer," and some have said I'm more of a "family man defenceman" just doing what it takes for the team. I see myself more as a natural goal-scoring, stay-at-home defenceman, offensive-threatening enforcer. So, basically, the most well-rounded player out there, to put it into layman's terms.

It was during the Bangladesh Pro and Virgin Islands Elite Annual Cross-League Match-Up where Olly and I first met. With a fresh sheet between us, the stare-down began, bench to bench. When we finally hit the ice on the same shift, we knew some kind of magic was about to happen. It was showtime for the two best players on the ice, and the score needed to be settled immediately. Olly could see I was a killer D-man, and when he flicked the biscuit into the corner and charged full speed expecting to nail me, I dropped a low hippie, sending him head-over-wheels into the glass. The crowd erupted—and not even ten seconds into the shift, the finger pillows were off.

Both of us knew we could each have had at least six points that night, and everyone in the stands believed it, too. But scrapping was the only way to settle this score. We went toe-to-toe, exchanging shots to the booger bag. Fists were flying, buckets popped off, and the crowd went crazy. After no less than 72 punches each, the zebras finally broke it up. The first go-around ended in a tie, so we knew we had unfinished business. After serving our time in the sin bin, we got on the ice for round two. The result was about the same as round one, though. At the end of the game, after 14 fights and 14 ties, we discovered we'd each met our match, and there was mutual respect between a couple of legends. Some people say those 14 fights and 212 punches will go down in history as racking up the longest scoresheet ever recorded.

Now that you know a little bit more about me and Olly, and understand why you should be taking our advice, let's spread some mayonnaise on a few fundies. Buckle up, boys: the pages are about to get greased.

2 THE GREATEST GAME

The game of puck is inarguably the greatest of all sports. It requires mastering speed, acing agility, and pushing beyond physical exhaustion every time you play—all while balancing on a pair of blades. This easily makes hockey the greatest game in the world. Anyone who thinks otherwise can, quite frankly, kick pucks.

So, how did the greatest game begin? That's easy: it was actually invented in our backyards. That's right, you can thank the Postanins and Ardowns for creating the great Canadian pastime, which forged a nation of puck players.

Jacob's ancestors played the very first game of hockey. Sir Alfred Mackenzie Peter Purenet Ardown paved the way, forging a legacy of legends. It is rumoured that Jacob's skill and hockey sense are largely based on the fact that hockey is literally running through his veins.

The game of hockey began in 1899, somewhere between what is known today as Vulcan, Alberta, and the Bay of Fundy near Nova Scotia and New Brunswick. It started with the early players in a shootout-type game where skaters used four- to five-foot sticks to push a frozen beaver tail past the goalkeeper, better known today as the "tendy." It was a first-to-50 game and matches could last up to seven hours.

The first hockey match involved the great Sir Alfred Ardown, who was both captain and coach of his team. The team was down early in the first period, so Sir Alfred himself initiated what is still the most used slash in the game: the Overhead Axe Chop. He broke nearly all the opponent's twigs, giving his team the upper hand and granting them the first win in the history of hockey.

Meanwhile, on the other side of the Bay of Fundy, a man named Sir Barret Bennet Twigtwister Johnson Postanin IV was also shootin' puck on a frozen sheet. He quickly got word there were other men using sticks to play a game of deke the tendy with a frozen beaver tail. Naturally, he challenged Sir Alfred to a match.

Each team used a three-man system with their biggest player as the tendy. The game went on all night—in fact, it lasted two-and-a-half days straight. Neither team was willing to stop or even admit they needed a break. They were born to play. Both teams believed they were the inventors of hockey, and pride wouldn't let either back down. They played on one of the largest lakes in the area. This made for a long skate for each team to rip the crisp beaver tail between the pipes.

Toward the end of day one, with both teams driven to win, things began to get a little rough. The Postanins started to thread their twigs between the feet of the Ardowns, which resulted in bodies hitting the ice hard. The Ardowns weren't about to concede and "the twig in skates" move only agitated them further. The next time one of the Postanins tried to thread wheels, Sir Ardown himself came out of nowhere with the first c-check in the history of the game. The grueling match ended when, days later, the Ardowns scored the lone goal. The game was called so both families could finally get some sleep.

Only after this game did teams implement the concept of penalties. The rules and regulations were modified in 1917, and all teams agreed to adhere to the new system. Thus was born the good, old-fashioned, clutch-and-grab physical game of puck we know today.

The lineages of the Ardowns and Postanins have been gracing the hockey world ever since their first epic match. In fact, the Postanins upped the ante by providing the very first championship cup to be won at the end of the year.

It was 1917 and Sir Barret Postanin hosted the month-long tournament. The teams played one game a day for the entire month of February, and at the end of the month, the team with the most wins took home the cup. The tourney and trophy were appropriately named the Sir Barret Bennet Twigtwister Johnson Postanin IV Cup. Once again, this maverick of the game made his mark, this time by giving teams something to play for.

As it was his tournament, Sir Barret Postanin decided that he would monitor and enforce all the rules of each game, even those his own team was playing in. Unsurprisingly, the Postanins won the tourney due to heavily biased reffing. Shortly after it ended, everyone complained about how the rules were enforced, so it was agreed that future matches would have their own unbiased officials.

As if that wasn't enough, he also invented the goal nets. These nets became the standard and were used in game-play for over 60 years. Handcrafted from corral doors his henchmen would scoop from farms across the land, each net was perfectly measured at 4×6. It is rumoured that he developed these dimensions to maximize both scoring as well as injury. By keeping the net smaller, there was a larger chance of the tendy getting hit.

The Ardowns and Postanins are the only documented families to have generations of hockey players that hearken back to the formulation of the game. The Ardown name boasts an impressive eight generations at the pro level, with each successive generation completing longer professional stints.

The Postanin name has an impressive 82 players of seven generations at the pro level. This is due to very large families. From 1926 to 1941, an eager

Postanin family created a whole team of Postanin children. In their 15 years of attempting to win with a family team, they only won a single game. Following the win, the family retired the team and the younger players joined other clubs, playing against family members for the first time.

The latest generation of Ardowns and Postanins are the ones you know and love today: Jacob Ardown and Olly Postanin. And, like our ancestors, we've surfaced from our private training facilities to change the game again.

The game is becoming less physical and faster, and we need to remember the day when you had to be tough and skilled to survive for any length of time. Because we have hockey in our blood, we possess skills that are second-to-none and far superior to anyone who has ever played. But the good news for you is that we are generous and want to share our knowledge.

The keys to success for any player are the fundies, and we are devoted to teaching them. Don't be fooled, though—you probably will never come close to our level. But keep in mind that even though we are way better than you, we are even more humble. We're also the best at being humble.

That's right, boys—we're humble legends!

3 DRESSING FOR PUCK

PLAYERS

You can't play puck without the right gear—that's a no-brainer. Each and every piece is just as important as the next. And there a few different things to look at when selecting your battle armour. Naturally, it would make sense to go from top to bottom, so we're going to talk about your cup first.

Now I know you're confused because I said we'd start at the top, so why aren't we talking about the bucket? My guess is that you struggle with pull-and-peel cheese strings, so I figured you would get lost. But get it together and follow along. Your cup is the absolute, most crucie part of the gear, so it sits at the top of the list. Protecting the jewels is job number one. If you remember in the eppie on blocking biscuits, Jacob laced up the ol' jock shorts and it basically saved his life. Remember, boys, keep that cup updated. Unlike your buckets, cups have expiry dates and replacing them regularly is an absolute must. The most important gear always has expiry dates.

The next piece of quitty you want to focus on is the wheels. Everyone knows that you can't play without wheels. There isn't a lot to choosing your ice melters, just find the flashiest ones out there. You need something that the scouts are going to notice. You want to be the one-man show that every scout is looking for, and flashy wheels will slingshot you well ahead of any other player.

Next on the list, you guessed it, are the chin seekers. If you don't know what these are, then you're probably into soft sports like basketball, where the worst injury is a jammed nose picker. The chin seekers are your standard set of elbow pads. It's not a good idea to get new ones often. You want to find a set that is already crusty, so they grip onto your skin and doesn't slide down your arms when you're hunting. If the lost-and-found bins are empty and you have to get fresh ones, no worries. We have tricks for that, too.

What you want to do is put a couple drops of maple syrup—the Canadian remedy for everything—right there on the inner padding, and toss 'em in the freezer for about an hour. Then wear them for a full day. Take them through showers, work, whatever you gotta do. That should help get a good crusting on them.

The only other thing to keep in mind when getting elbies is go for the biggest caps, but the shortest overall length. Basically, you want a big piece of plastic covering the elbow bend and that's about it. The smaller the pad, the more movement you have for dishin' folded fives to the booger bag. The plastic caps are there to add a few extra stitches in some benders.

Next, you need to dress the ol' popsicle sticks. Shinnies and pants go together. That's because you only need to wear them to match the rest of the team. Shinnies are there to fill up the socks. They don't really serve a purpose, but it looks cooler than a couple popsicle sticks coming out of a bobble top, like football players. When you are looking at shinnies, boys, just get the cheapest and flimsiest, so they don't affect you burnin' hoof.

And now, the bucket. First things first: bird cage over bubble every time. Unless you hate breathing, then toss a big old windshield over that mug shot and suck some slew water. The biggest beauties are going no face shields. Less quitty means more speed. It's easy geology!

I guess we can toss shouldies into the mix now. Simply put, you don't need them. If you want them, then figure it out.

TENDIES

Picking out the right gear as a tendy is pretty simple. The most basic fundy is getting the biggest quitty they have. The chest protector alone should take up over half the net. Your pads should stack up to half the height of the net, too. And remember, plain pillows are cool pillows. They blend with the mesh of the ol' 4×6, making it harder to find the holes to snipe at. This goes for your glove and catcher, too: keep 'em simple. Your saves will make them look flashy enough, if you're any good.

If you want colour, your bucky is where that comes in. Pick the coolest designs and get custom wraps any chance you can. Only wear the cat-eye style cages. Even though you aren't allowed to wear them until you're in the show, just do it because they look way cooler. That's about it for tendy gear. Get it big—that's the most soups-crucial thing.

THE T.J.

Not sure what that is? It stands for tape job, one of the most important things for a player to have. A good T.J. will separate you from the other plugs. You want your twig to look like a fresh Christmas present, and it should be an extension of the type of player you are.

The best T.J.s make a statement. Ones like the Candy Cane, Mummy, Euro special, Iron Cross, Hilly Heel, and J-Benn will help you stand out. Each T.J. is going to benefit certain shots differently.

The Candy Cane is going to get those wristies and backies off your twig fast and high. This is a simple T.J. that looks incredible and sets you apart from everyone else. The front of the blade will have three stripes of tape going up and down. The back of the blade also has three stripes running up and down but with a diagonal line connecting each straight line, making for the perfect candy cane T.J. Skilled players use this to draw more attention to themselves. It is perfect tape art to attract the scouties to you.

The Mummy is the perfect T.J. for the sniper on the team. More tape means more control of the bisccy, and better accuracy when shooting.

The Highlighter seems simple, but it is possibly the easiest one to mess up because of the inclination to keep adding tape. You just want to use the tape around the edge of your blade, highlighting the most important part of the twig. Goal-scorers and master playmakers use this T.J.

The Toey is exactly what it sounds like: one loop around the toe of the blade. This T.J. is for the boys that toe-drag everything, so the only move you're going to want to try with this TJ is the toe-drag to quick snapper. The players with this T.J. typically don't have any other shots in their arsenal.

The Iron Cross is a gorgeous T.J. that rockets appreciate. Start in the middle on the back and do a full loop along the length of the blade, coming back to where you started. Press your thumb into the tape and now change directions, making one full loop around the height of the blade, finishing again at the same spot you started on the back. It's an easy technique and one of the best T.J.s you can do.

The Hilly Heel is an excessive amount of tape put right on the heel of the blade, which is going to push the puck to the toe, making your snapper extra greasy and quick. Instead of shooting with the middle of the twig, you want to hit the bisccy on the hill of the heel. This will start the bisscy spinning to speed burst it off the toe, increasing your shot power by a minimum 0.139%.

Named for Jamie Benn, everyone knows **The J-Benn** is for the players that dominate and just don't care. This is where you have tape only in the middle of the blade—anywhere from one loop to a maximum three loops. Simple and effective, it says that you do what you want, when you want. It also shows exactly where to rip a clapper from.

The Spidey Web isn't a very common T.J., but it is extremely effective. It extends from the toe of the twig to about five inches up the shaft from the blade. Start on the blade with the Mummy and then create the web from the toe to the shaft. This T.J. is perfect for knocking down passes, keeping the puck in the zone, and tipping in shots in front of the tendy.

OLLY

One of
game is
weapon
makes th
possibilit
dome.

The signat
shoulder-le
classic look
styles. Every
enforcer han
massages. It
in the game. Y
flop. It's versat
bread after a g

Then there's the
usually 'cause yc
haircuts and just
the scrappers. Ha
head keeps your
toe. The guy you a
on to, unless you h
good ol' Jumbo Jo

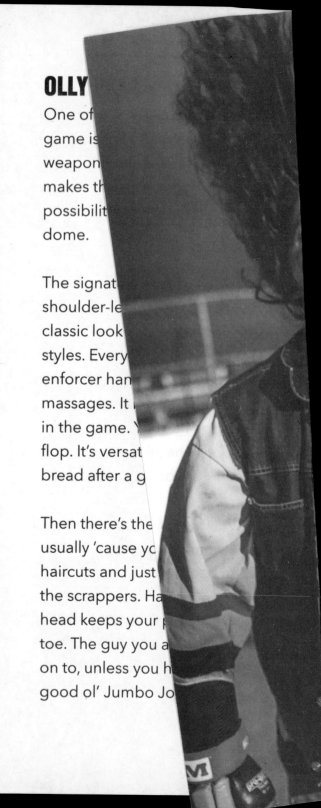

chin grab from Nazem Kadri was tough to watch.) The buzz is also easy-care, which is nice when you want to get out fast for some wobbly pops with the boys.

We can't forget the standard crew. This chop is another all-time classic. A little spike up at the front and you're ready to go anywhere. The boys rockin' this leather sweatsuit of a mop chop are your blue-collar boys: third liners going to work. Getting in there and really muckin' barn in the corners. Hackin' away at some garbage goals and not afraid to shed 'em and teach anyone a lesson. Every once in a while, they even play a little pipe music, rippin' some missies off the iron and straight down. Followed up, naturally, with the subtle celly and chirps that cut like daggers.

Last and most crucial is the mullet (pronounced moo-lay in Canadian). A legendary style that isn't for everyone. It bears a huge amount of responsibility. Jaromir Jagr is the true avatar and leader of this flop. Pure style in the front, going either Kelly Hrudey comb-over or standard crew. But the back flows, the breeze from smooth skating sending it on a ride. It is arguably the most poetic chop. This hair belongs on two types of players. The first is obvious: if you play like Jagr, you can rock it. But you can't play like Jagr. So, you can be the reckless-abandon player. The type of player that only has one gear. A pure overdrive, sandbag wheeler, full-boar, and no-brakes on either 30 minutes or ten hours of sleep, kind of player. These are heart-and-soul players that get you in every door you always dreamt of going through. The mullet is not for the faint of heart, boys. It is lethal in all aspects. Put it this way: if you even have to ask if you should rock it, the answer is no.

For some guys, the lettuce always changes. It's just whatever's hot at the time. The boys with the trendy mops are typically your goal-scorers or top producers—and, of course, the tendies. These boys are usually the first ones to pump their own tires. Every pick-up line they have involves at least one of their stats from the best season they played.

JACOB ARDOWN ON FLOW MAINTENANCE

We've established the significance of good flow, but we're not done. Once you've locked the look, there's maintenance, boys. When we're talking about maintaining the flow, we don't just mean the loaf on top of the dome. We mean the beards and muzzies, too, the whole dome upholstery. The styles you pick deserve the best upkeep. Find a routine and stick to it. For example, if you are a greasy player, it's a no-brainer for you. Get it greased right back and use all the right oils on the chin curtains and lip sweaters to make them shine. You want your level of greasiness to be reflected in your mint-condition, 1982 shag face carpet.

Now, since I have the deadliest lettuce in the game, I'll let you in on some of my secrets for maximum flow. First, never brush it. That's the Jacob Ardown number one rule. Flow like this doesn't poof with a brush weeding it out. Get your digits going through it and that's it.

Second, no showering within 24 hours of a game or event. You want the flop to shine like that lucky rod in your left ankle.

Third, and super crucie: NO FUN BUNS! Putting your feather bucket up is like leaving your skate guards on to hit the ice, only you would likely have more success skating on wheel guards.

Basically, you just want to make it as greasy as possible, boys. Always let the flow flop and don't hold 'er back!

TOP 5 TWIGS

1. **The Aluminum:** The Great One used this bad boy. No flex, no grip, super heavy. As close to perfect as you can get.
2. **The Classic 5030:** Made from the best wood you have ever had in your hand. Perfect rubber rockets.
3. **The Z-bubble:** The classic compy two-piece—this thing was art!
4. **The Hespeler:** Literally no one knows how to say it and that makes it cool.
5. **The Titan:** If you never tried a Titan woody, then you really missed out.

They're nearly impossible to find
now, and even more difficult to
stop shots from.

This list is not in any order, just five of our faves
throughout the years. Jacob actually broke 38
Z-bubbles with his aluminum twig back in the day,
throwin' slashies and flooding the scoresheet. Now
that's a stat worth remembering!

4 GENERAL RULES

Hockey is much more than a game of pushing a biscy across a sheet and serving it to a tendy. It's certainly not as easy as we make it look. There are a couple rules in the game that are super crucial to understand. You'll never be as good as us, but start with these few guidelines of play and you should at least understand where you fall short.

NEUTRAL ZONE

To understand the fundies better, you need to know more about the game as a whole. The rink is divided into three different zones. First is the neutral zone. This is where the game starts. It's the area between the blueys. This area is kind of a safe spot of the ice for either team. No one should really score from here. Except Olly and Jacob, of course, since we have the power to send the biscy from anywhere on the sheet. If the puck by chance does go in the net from the neutral zone, then it is for sure the tendy's fault. For all you tendies reading this, when someone tells you that it wasn't your fault, they are lying to you. It most definitely was your fault.

The neutral zone is used for picking up speed. When you're burnin' hoof up the wall, this area is where you have to toss it into overdrive and cook it. If you take it slow, one of your teamies is probably going to throw you offside (we'll get to that). Your biggest neutral zone fundy is this: you don't want to get a pass in this area. Taking a pass in the neutral zone is going to put you into suey position and really open you up for a Scott Stevens hit. Sending passes is okay, though, because it won't be you getting hit. Actually, it's a good move. After your teamie has taken the flattening, you can scoot over, pick the bisccy back up, and head down for a low-cheese missy.

DEFENSIVE ZONE

The D-zone is the second most important zone. This is the area from your tendy to your bluey. You don't want the other team to have the puck here because they might score on you. And if you haven't figured it out yet, the whole point of hockey is trying to score more goals than the other team. So, when you are in the D-zone, you want to get the puck first. If there's a chance of you getting hammered into the boards, pull your parachute out and lock up the brakes. That way the meathead trying to clobber you will zoom past, and you can hear all the wind leaving his body from one end or the other.

When you get the bisccy in your end, first thing you want to do is get it out. Ideally, you want to skate coast-to-coast and try for that highlight reel goal. Scouties are looking for leaders and flashy players that can score the greasy goals. Sometimes you will be forced to pass, though. Almost all coaches say not to pass the puck up the middle in the D-zone. Everyone knows that. So you should pass right through the middle because no one thinks you will. Strategy is key in this area of the ice. While you're at it, make those passes cross the ice through the D-zone, too. It will open it up even more, so you can burn hoof and get the puck back and head in for a snizz.

OFFENSIVE ZONE

Obviously, the O-zone is the most important part of the ice. Why? That's simple: this is where you snipe top corns, or tuck in a quick wrappy. The O-zone is between the other team's bluey and their tendy. It's also their D-zone. In this area, the only thing you should be thinking about is getting on the scoresheet, so keeping the puck on your twig is vital. Passing in the O-zone isn't really recommended because you may not get the puck back. What you want to do instead is keep the puck and make as many moves as possible before going for a snipe. Don't take the easy shot either —you have to dress it up and make it worthwhile. The chances of it ending up in the scoutie's hands are better when you open up the jar of mayo on it and really grease it. In short, the O-zone is where you are thinking only about yourself and what you can do to tickle twine.

OFFSIDE

This rule is soups crucial to the flow of the game. To stay onside, the puck must cross over your offensive blue line before any of your players do (including you, so simmer down there, bud). This means you can dump it in or skate it in as long as the puck gets across the bluey before any of your team's feet crosses it. If you don't understand this, you will cause the linesman to blow the whistle, toss his chicken wing up in the air, and stop play. So if your team has a full head of momentum rolling through the neutral zone, make sure you aren't the one causing the offside.

It's probably the simplest rule in the game. Just remember, offside equals whistle and onside equals no whistle.

We feel like you're struggling trying to keep up with this. Let's try this: do you play soccer in the summer? If you do, you should stop. Play lacrosse or something cool. If you're going to learn how to dive, then take swimming lessons. Now that has nothing to do with soccer or offsides—we just felt we needed to get that off our chest.

ICING

No, we are not talking about icing on a cake. That's not a funny joke, so please stop making it. When you hear "that's icing," it should tell you that the biscuit has travelled too long a distance over the ice surface. Honestly, it should be self-explanatory.

Icing is when you rip the bisccy from your side of the centre line and the puck crosses the goal line in the other team's D-zone. Even if you are only an inch from the centre line and you go for the ol' dump and grease, if the puck crosses the goal line, the whistle is blown and the face-off comes back to your end of the ice. That means if you're standing beside your goalie and rip a clapper, trying to pick off one of the other team's D-men, but miss and the puck goes all the way down the ice, crossing the goal line by the other team's goalie, you're getting the icing call. So don't miss that blueliner.

Also, you have to keep in mind that when your team gets the icing call, you're not allowed to change lines. A lot of people see this as a bad thing, but they don't know the fundies. Next time Coach Cheese-knees is screaming at you to get off the ice because your normal two-minute shift is getting closer to the three-minute mark, just flip that bisccy deep down the sheet and enjoy some more ice time. You've earned it.

Here's a pro tip since you've mastered icing now. So you are on your side of the centre line and you want to get that puck deep without getting a whistle. If someone touches the puck between you and the goal line, then icing is waved off. Plus you get a chance to run over a defenceman on the way into the zone. Also, if you get the puck on net and the tendy stops it, then it's not icing. If the tendy doesn't stop it, then you just sniped a snizzy from 200 feet away. Make sure to celly hard.

We can't really break it down any more than that. If you are still having trouble, then maybe soccer is your sport.

SECRET PLAY: OPENING FACE-OFF

Coaches everywhere are always trying to come up with secret plays to get the upper hand in a game. Since you got this book and are obviously a fan and believer of the fundies, we are going to let you in on our most secretest of plays that we like to run. This play is called "the blitz."

Typically, you only want to use this play on the opening face-off, but you can use it at the start of

any period if you need to change the momentum. DO NOT use this play at any other point in a game. And don't try to modify it or change it—we know what we're doing and it is perfect the way it is. Not to mention you struggle at taking selfies, so let us teach the play. Here's how it goes.

Centremen, you have the most important job. As soon as that puck drops, you have to tie up the other bender's stick. Just leave the bisccy sitting there. Take one or two strides forward to push that plug away from the face-off dot. Wingers, listen up: you have a super-crucial part to play now. As soon as the rubber hits the ice, carve a half moon into the pigeon you're lined up against—hold them there on the outside.

Defence, you are the bread and toast to this play. The other defence is going to scramble toward the bisccy. But that's okay because this is where the blitz comes in. Both of you are going wide, like real wide, and get those hoofs burning straight away. Get the crossies going strong as you hit the bluey and start turning in toward the tendy at the face-off dots. You both want to make contact with the tendy at the same time.

The whole point of this play is to get the back-up tendy in early. If you are out in warmies and the other squad is lookin' fresh, you need to find a way to give your team the upper hand. This is the perfect play. No one will see it coming and they won't have a clue how to respond. Then you can start snizzing and filling the scoresheet!

LINE CHANGE AND SHIFT LENGTH

The change is short and sweet, boys. Line changes are always board hops. As for your shift, length is minimum two minutes. The longer your shifts are, the better chance you have of snizzing. And you also get to show how good your stamina is.

POWER PLAY: MAN UP, STATS UP

A power play, also known as the PP, is when the other team has a penalty. Your team plays with all five skaters while the other team only has four skaters on the ice. You always want to try and get on the man advantage. If you get onto the PP, the only thing you want to focus on is scoring. Don't worry about the breakout, you have more players than the other team right now, so it should be super easy to get into their zone. There are hundreds of different systems to use on the PP, but they don't matter. Just make sure you are always in the one-T position. Every time the bisccy comes your way, you're pulling the trigger. Slapshot everything. Try to shoot as hard as you can, so it's either going in or, if you miss the net, it's ripping around the boards and eliminating the chance of someone else scoopin' your snizz.

The PP is all about adding to your stats. The penalty timer on the scoreboard lets you know how long your shift should be—try to get out for the whole penalty. It is the perfect time to be selfish. With fewer players on the ice, the scouties will have an easier time seeing you, so just focus on getting the snizz!

THE PK (NOT SUBBAN)

The penalty kill is more for the coach's pet type of players. The ones that want to block shots and just ice the bisccy, typically. And on the PK, you don't get a whistle for icing, so if you're a no-talent duster and want to suck up to the clipboard carrier, you can probably at least do that. A lot of players think of it the wrong way and fall into this typical routine. Remember, if you get tossed out for the PK, you don't have to be a coach's pet. With one less player to pass to, room will open up to skate. This is your chance to take 'er end-to-end and rip rope on a slick shorty! Any short-handed goal is a pretty one, and the more shorties you get, the more scouties are going to look at you.

There isn't a whole lot to the PK. No one really wants to be on it, and we don't blame them. If you try to focus on getting a shorty, though, it'll help. If you get scored on, it doesn't really count against you either. Those goals only go against the tendies. Since there are fewer bodies on the ice, it should be even easier to see the puck and make the save. Yup, tendy's fault for sure.

MEAT TOSSIN' (BODY CHECKS)

There are plenty of different ways to chuck your meat around. Trying to get you to understand every single way is nearly impossible. Since we are such great guys, though, we will look at a couple of ways you can run a train through the station.

First things first: what is the object of a body check? Coaches are going to tell you it's to separate the man from the bisccy. That's ridiculous. The guys saying that would likely float around the ice and pick cherries before going anywhere near a good corner muckin'. The simple truth is the purpose of tossing around your meat is total and absolute destruction. The boards should shake, and the goal should always be to shatter some glass. Yeah, you're going to separate the man from the puck, but don't worry about the bisccy. A better way to look at it is to separate the man from the play. By taking him out of the equation, and jumping right back into the play yourself, you give your team the upper hand. More often than not, though, you want to stick around and celly over the pile. Cellys aren't just for goals, boys. The more you celly throughout a game, the more visible your name bar is, which ultimately gets you scouted.

HIPPIE

Obviously, boys, the hippie is the best hit to make in hockey. If you don't agree with that, then you should find a different sport. Understanding the fundies of tossing a mean hippie is super crucial to being a great player.

The first thing you need to work on is the knee bend. You want to have them bent as much as your ankles do. Think of the biggest duster with cheese strings for ankles and make your knees bend like that. The lower you get, the better your hippie will be. When you're going to roast some toast, you want your speed up and the hip tucked —get your backside almost on the ice. By lowering your body this way, you ensure that contact occurs in between the kneecap and hip flexor.

This is the prime territory to target to get a full flip in on the hippie.

After dialing in the height, you want to then focus and perfect what we call "the springboard." It should be self-explanatory, but since we have a bunch of dusters muckin' up the pages, we will explain it to you. To execute the perfect springboard, you want to activate the launch button when your victim is parallel to the ice over your back. Use their momentum and a slight pitchfork with the elbow to really assist this effort. When you feel the enemy rolling over your back, lock those knees and bounce up like a back-up dancer in the worst rap video you've ever seen. The faster you get those knees straight and locked, the greater the height. You're going for a fully devastating front flip here.

It seems like a simple task, but to get the right springboard will take years of praccy. We recommend hitting the O.D.R. with your siblings or friends for a friendly game of sticks in the middle. Once the action gets going, it's time to praccy. You want to hit them when they're not expecting it, for maximum effect. Playing the one-on-one, get nice and low and find a soft pillow of fresh snow to send them into. The more times you do this, the easier it will be in an actual game—and the better your chances of getting scouted. Scouties love the hippie, boys.

Now we have the height and springboard sorted out, it's time to understand the speed at which a hippie should be sent. The main point to remember is you are always going full send. Get your speed up. A bunch of crossies is really going to help you out here. For all of you that can't skate backwards, well, this hit isn't for you. So get those rudders figuring out how to skate in rewind and then reread this chappy. Now, with the crossies going strong, you have a full wind-up and you're tucked in high gear. Use the two blueys as your gauge. Start from your offensive zone and back-pedal all the way to your defensive zone bluey. This should be plenty of time to build up speed and line up your target. Now it's time to get the knees tucked and the springboard ready. A good hippie is going to look like art. It can be something magical if you get it right. And if you time it right, you can send a full bend over your back and into the crowd or players' benches.

Never take this hit for granted and never let your guard down. Falling for a hippie is not going to get you scouted or even on the scoresheet. It will, however, leave you benched. Coaches don't want a player doing flips like a circus act. You need to be putting people in the circus!

SHOULDY

After mastering the hippie, you need to perfect a good shouldy. Obviously, you want to make contact with the top of your chicken wing. When you are aiming for a good shouldy, you want to key in on a specific target on the body for maximum effect. Otherwise, going shouldy-on-shouldy is a very standard hit. Either way, the shouldy should plank your victim, sending him sides and parallel with the ice before letting frostbite take over. And if you aim for the numbies, it makes for a lethal hit. Remember, a little speed goes a long way. Numbies are a fun targgy. At the point of contact, you can lock up your brakes and toss it in park to watch the devastation. The important thing here is don't limit yourself. Anything is fair game when you are rolling through like a sledgehammer.

C-CHECK

There's no check like a c-check. It's a huge part of puck. Flexin' your biscuit ripper over some plug feels so natural. It's kind of like feeling your wheels light up the ice for the first time. It's almost calming, like yoga, except it's violent.

The c-check is an art that takes time to perfect. Don't expect the first one you toss to work exactly how you want. You will need to practise these

every chance you get. So when you're shovelling the driveway and the mailman is walking by, forget what you're doing and lay him out. When you're sweeping the floor, doing your chores before Mom gets home, and your dad walks around the corner, you bet he's chest bumping a broom handle.

To unleash a good c-check, there are some super-important things to work on. First thing to think about is your grip. When lining up to send one, you want a nice wide grip. Get your bottom hand just a little lower than it would be for a clapper, so it's sitting just above the blade of your twig. Lining up like this will allow a few different things. You will achieve maximum flex. The more you flex your rubber ripper, the better chance you have of breaking it. When you can break your twig over some cheese wheel, you know you have successfully completed the perfect c-check. Another reason to have your grip like this is to minimize any chance of missing. With the most surface area available on your twig, you have a better chance of making contact even if the greaser is moving around. If he tries to hit you with a stutty step and curl around, with a nice wide grip you can catch him with one end or the other, depending on which way he goes. If you don't crack him dead centre on your twig, you won't get it to break, but you can still serve him dead arms and make him think twice the next time he tries to go around you.

The next thing you want to focus on is your stance. For a standing-still c-check, you want to keep your wheels apart and bend the knees before striking. The lower you start, the more power you will have coming up through buddy's cheeseburger holder. If you want to knock him down, you'll need all the power you have coming straight through. Keep the twig moving forward and upward at 45 degrees, and the duster will be parking himself on the ice in less than a second, easily. If you are hand delivering a c-check when you're moving, you want to pick up some speed. Throw in a couple of crossies and fully extend your wings well before impact. This technique requires little to no arm movement and is one of the deadliest c-checks and fastest ways to the sin bin.

The last thing to think about for a solid c-check is your wrists. They need to be locked in. Get yourself some 28 gloves like we wear to really help you out. There's absolutely no way you will be able to dangle with them, but that's because you are nowhere near as good as we are. If you let those wrists wobble like your ankies do, then there is absolutely no way that you will ever toss a solid c-check. So, lock 'em in nice and tight, just like the rock piles lock in the water bottle lids.

DOUBLE FISTER

The last type of hit we want to talk about is the double fister. If this weren't a book, we would ask what you think it is just to prove how much you don't actually know. Though it doesn't really matter what you think. The double fister is quite simple. Basically, you want to head through your targgy with both your fists tucked into your chest, bracing yourself for the hit. When you make contact in this fashion, it limits the chances of you going down and greatly increases the chance of the plugs taking a ride on the cold slip-and-slide. The biggest factor to this is speed. Wind 'er up nice and fast, set your sights early, and fully commit. A hit like this should be thunderous. It will also undoubtedly earn you more ice time.

TAKIN' A HIT

Throwing the body around is pretty effortless when you get going; all you do is steamroll people. Being able to take a hit, though, is a little different, and something most people aren't taught anymore. This is a prime example of why you need us. If you don't know a hit is coming, then whatever happens, happens.

Taking a hit seems simple enough, but there's more to it than you know. When you see a freight train coming at you, there's a couple different things you can do depending on where the goon is coming from.

If a player is coming in hot from the side, that's easy: get the bows up into the side of the dome and they will think twice the next time. Or turn your numbies to him right before he hits you. The best way to take a hit is to also draw a penalty. When you get rolled over, just tuck yourself and summersault out of it. The plug will go to the sin bin, and you will get your chance to repay him with a top corns ripper.

If he's coming head-on, the best option is the c-check brace. Get both hands up and try to clothesline the sucker around the shoulders. Another good one for a head-on hit is the turtle. Exactly how it sounds, just duck nice and low and let them go right over top.

Now if you have someone hot on your tail and he's going to try to run numbies, hit him with the canny (or can-opener). All you have to do is lock the brakes up and lean hard, putting your shoulder through this guy's chest.

There is another option, though, and this one everyone always forgets about. When you know you aren't going to be able to stand 'em up with a canny, get those knees locked straight and stand as tall as you can. You are for sure going to take the fall, but you probably won't feel it and that's the main point to take from this.

The last way to take a hit we want to look at is the Overhead Axe Stop. This more than likely is going to get the buster burnin' hoof on you to pull out the parachute and retreat. So when you are feeling the pressure and can see 'em running straight for

you, you want to get your twig way up behind your back. When they're about three or four feet from you, swing your twig fast and hard down. When he sees this, he will flinch for sure and grease the brake peddy, leaving you unscathed.

PIMS

Understanding the fundies of PIMs will make your career in the league more memorable—that's the key here. Once your hockey career is over, you want the boys to look back and remember the kinda beaut you were, and PIMs is where it starts.

There's a lot of bennys to taking PIMs, boys. You're probably thinking that doesn't seem right, that if you take a penalty, you're putting your team down a man. That's true, but you're also helping them develop into better players by giving them more ice time.

But this is about you, and the reason you wanna take a penalty in normal games is to let the scouties know that you're here to play, that you're ready to do what it takes to win. Once the scouties see you run a plug from behind, straight through the numbies, they're gonna know you mean business.

There are times in the game where you're going to want to turn a two into a ten. These times will come often, boys. When you're in a big game and things aren't going your way and you're down by a few, this is when you wanna pick up a ten.

This will get you out of the game faster—you don't wanna be in a game when the boys are getting blown out. Leave as soon as possible, so it's not your fault the boys lost. Here's an easy one: unsportsmanlike. This is a great one because you can chirp the ref 'til he boots you. This also lets the boys hear your nasty chirps, which will 100 percent intimmy the other team.

SLASHIES

To be a top-notch hockey player, it is super crucial to know how to get on the scoresheet. You know we preach about flooding it, but we don't mean just with points. Penalties are just as important. A solid two-hand chop is the easiest way to get on the parade to the box.

There are a few key areas to target with a slash. The most important place is the shin pads of the other dust bag. If you swing for the fences against someone's rudder, the zebras are sure to hear it. Even if they don't see the thunderous slash, you should be able to buckle the knee enough to drop him down. When the stripes see him wincing, they'll get their chicken wing in the air, sending you to the office for a two-minute coffee break.

Another great spot to target is the top of the laces. This is more for close quarter slashing. When you are in the corners muckin' barn, the ice piggies' eyes are going to be glued to the play. You won't have to use the big wind-up here, so attack the laces. It's a tender area, so a little lightning quick chop will work nicely to get that penalty.

Outside of those areas, the only other spot you want to try to get is the twig, boys. Right near the digits. Get the lumber down on the finger pillows and they will let go and start giving their face massagers a shake, as if that will actually make the pain go away. As soon as the refs see this motion, they know exactly what's happened, and again your parade to the box begins. If you end up missing the mitts of the bender you are hacking, then you will get their twig—and if you come down hard enough, you can break it. This is the double-double: not only do you get on the scoresheet, but he has to get his mom to buy him a new one after the game. Or wherever sticks come from.

Slashing is very straightforward. It's similar to a standard clapper, but instead of making a half circle on the downswing for a shot, you are coming straight down on the target.

HOOKING

Looking for the easiest way to speed up your wheels? Sending out a fishing line on a heavy hook will help you a lot. Twisting your wood up in some bender's gut and leaning back will really propel you, and also conserves your energy. If you pull hard with your chicken wings, you can send yourself forward, speeding up to either get the bisccy or make a bone-crushing hit. As a bonus, hooking is also an easy trip to the box for a two-minute rest.

Hooking is a super-straightforward fundy to get the hang of. The focus of a solid hook is where to latch on. If you are right behind someone on a b-way and you are trying to stop them from getting off a good shot and possibly snizzing, your hook should be placed at an elbow. This way, when you lock up the brakes and make that long haul backwards, you can rip a mitt off the twig, stopping any chance of a shot getting off.

In any other situation, focus on hooking the gut or right under the armpit. If you are feeling gassed or even just lazy, then this hook is for you. Latch on, sit back, and just let that coach's pet pull you around the ice.

TRIPPING

This is one of the most used penalties. It's a go-to and extremely effective if you are any good at hockey. Some plugs think that you can trip using your legs, but that's ridiculous. Don't put your rudder on the line. Always use your twig if you are going to trip someone.

The best trip that works at least 100 percent of the time is called "threading your wood." It's all about timing. As your victim is skating, pick the perfect moment and slide your twig through his rudders, stopping his wheels as soon as they come into contact. Down he goes. When executed right, it looks like poetry.

A great time to use a trip is when you're battling anywhere on the ice. This trip is called "chuckin' hay bales." It's exactly how it sounds. Think of a

farmer tossing around bales with a pitchfork. Now your twig is the pitchfork and your victim's ankles are the hay bales. Lock in the blade of your rubber rocket with the top, thin side on the skate laces and pull back and up as hard as you can. If you can do it quickly, you might be able to make the dust bag look like a scorpion on the ice.

ELBOWING

We honestly shouldn't have to tell you much about this one. Get your chin seekers up and in the face of anyone near you, and you will get an elbowing penalty.

HIGH-STICKING

This is one of the best penalties to take. It can get you anything from a two-minute minor in the sin bin to a game ejection. It's pretty straightforward to understand. Any contact to anyone above the shouldies will result in a high-sticking penalty, and a nice two minute rest. If you draw blood, though, they can bump that up to four minutes. And if the zebras think you did it on purpose, good news: you get to hit the press box for some chicken fingies before any of the other boys.

To pull this off, skate pitchfork style with two hands on your wood, swinging it back and forth nice and high. Anyone that gets in the danger zone is going to get a mouth full of slivers. If the bisccy is up in the air above you, swing your rubber rocket around in an attempt to knock it down. Again, anyone that gets in the way of your twig is going to help get you on that scoresheet.

The stealthiest way to get a high-sticking award is when you go for that quick stick lift. If you got a plug that's been burning you all game and he's got the biscuit on his twig, go for the scoop up, underneath the heel of his twig. Try to send that thing to the moon as you go south to north, pulling the trigger all the way over your head. It's a good chance that you'll mash his booger bag and you bet you'll be hitting the scoresheet with that one.

INTERFERENCE

This one is fun. Well, it's fun if you are the one taking the penalty. It's straightforward: you'll earn an interference penalty every time you hammer someone who doesn't have the puck on their stick. Always play with the mindset that everyone is fair game at any point in time. If you think you're going to get beat to a loose puck, or someone cranked you last shift and they're a sitting duck, drop the shoulder and send 'em for a ride. Most of these penalties are going to happen away from the play, so you have to make sure the stripes are watching if you want a trip to the office. Bang your twig on the ice a couple times to get their eyes on you. As soon as you feel like you have an audience, move in for the strike.

FOLDED FIVES AND BOOGER BAGS

Scrappin' is one of the main parts of hockey. A lot of people think that fighting should be removed from the game. These are the same people that eat pizza with a knife and fork. They don't have a clue. Although you absolutely are trying to win and serve up more knuckle sandwiches than your opponent, it isn't about hurting someone. Fighting is about respect and can tone down a game when it's getting out of hand. So, as far as we are concerned, keep serving up hot batches of sucky soup!

Starting a good tilly takes a few key ingredients. You can't just shed the finger pillows and go out guns blazin'. And, on that point, getting the mitts off should take no more than two shakes. If it's three or more, then you're just playing with yourself. So now, gloves are on the ice and you have to go through the routine.

Always start in this exact way, so the other guy knows what's happening. Your face massagers are locked in place in front of your face, fists are loose, and as you move around, use your thumb from your jab hand to give the booger bag a wipe.

Immediately following the wipe, turn your head just slightly and give a little spit. Do not ever spit on anyone—this is a gentlemen's agreement now. The nose wipe and spit tell everyone around what's happening. Now it's time to exchange presents!

We just mentioned a "jab hand." Yeah, we know you have no clue what that means. We will explain it. Stop googling it or asking your dad. Your jab hand could be either your left or right depending on what way you line up. It could also change in a scrap if you can switch stances fast enough. Just remember, whichever hand is out the furthest is your jab hand. The most common stance is the standard righty. This means your power knuckles are your right hand, and your jab would be the lefty. Even though it's not the power punch, the jab can be how you win or lose. It is a speed hand, not only latching on to some squid's jersey but also tossing quick knucks in a nice methodic massage of the lower jawline up to the cheekbone area.

The power hand is going to be whichever hand you have furthest away from the opponent. Typically, this is the right hand—that's what we are going to refer to so we don't confuse you. Now, with the power hand you are looking to do a few things. Every strike from this hand is going to be a sledgehammer. Try not to miss your targgy or you might need a new shoulder. And get in as many uppies as you can, moving your arm like a jigsaw. If you slow the speed down a bit, you can increase the power.

You just couldn't help googling this, and now you're asking, "What's a southpaw?" A southpaw is someone who prefers sending sledgehammers with the left hand. So if you're preparing some sucky soup with your left and jabbing with the right, then you are a southpaw. It's a pretty simple concept—not too sure why you are struggling to understand it.

A lot of people outside the game of hockey think that scraping is just for violence and anger. That's absolutely ridiculous. The intent of a good donnybrook isn't to hurt anyone, it's to change the pace of the game. When two beauties square up for a two-step, there's always a reason. If someone gets hurt or receives a cheap shot, there should be a scrap. Not in an eye-for-eye situation, but to let the plugs know that you aren't going to back down.

Lots of stick work happening? Maybe the zebras on the fifth line aren't making the calls they should be. To change the flow of the game and cool down the cheap shots, the mitts are coming off like wrapping paper on Christmas morning. What about when your squad's down a couple and the energy just isn't there? Time for a yard sale, and all mitts are discounted! Fighting isn't about violence —it's about tempo and sticking up for yourself and your team.

DELAY OF GAME

We don't really like to use this penalty often because it slows the game down too much. Typically, the players who cause delays do so when they don't want to take any risks. Basically, this is when you know you aren't as good as your opponent, so you take a panic penalty.

As a player, the most common way to get a delay of game would be to rip the bisscy over the glass when you get in a tough spot. You could also cover the puck with your hand and get the stripes to blow it dead. Most of the time when you are taking these, it's because you're afraid to get hit.

Tendies can also take this penalty. Let's say some burner is heating up on a b-way coming straight at you. You've been getting lit up lately, so you aren't feeling confident about this easy save. Turn around and push the mesh cage off the goal line. As soon as the net moves, the stripes will blow the play dead. The benefit for the tendy is a teammate will go to the bin on your behalf. You hit the scoresheet and get to stay in the game.

Delay of game isn't a noble penalty like basically all the others. We do not recommend taking one, but if you're in a drought and need to get your name on the sheet, it's a surefire way to do so.

5 DO AND DON'T DO

FLOODING THE SCORESHEET

One of the most important fundies that we preach is flooding the scoresheet. Getting your number on the scoresheet as many times as possible is key to being a good player. Obviously, the main goal is to overload in the twine tickling department. Your number constantly embarrassing tendies is one of the most important things that scouties are looking for.

Getting on with some apples is good, too. Chuckin' some UFOs to a buddy to tuck in low cheese is for sure going to make the highlight reel. But our favourite way to hit the sheet is with penalties. Serving a two min. is good, but a ten min. is huge. Sacrificing everything for your team and getting penalties is a huge compliment you can pay to any coach.

CELLYS

This is a huge part of the game. Strong cellys are key to being a great player. After you absolutely embarrass the other team, you have to rub it in their faces. There is no wrong time to unleash a celly, but certain ones are best used in different situations.

Walking around defence and ripping one top corns calls for cellys like the harpoon and the twizzler. If you just had a deadly tic-tac-toe play, then a partner celly is in order—something like the line dance or the punt are great for these types of goals. Whatever you do, make sure they are flashy and well thought out. Everyone needs to know exactly what you are doing. Don't draw it out too long, though: short and sweet, so you can get back to ripping rubber.

The celly is one of the most important parts of hockey, boys, and it's not only for after you tickle twine. Cellys can be implemented into every aspect of your game. For example, in warmies when you blast a clapper bar down, toss in a little celly—maybe a glove flip or shoot an arrow into the stands. It doesn't matter what celly, as long as you pull one out.

Another perfect time to celly is after you toss a big hit. Once you crush some fourth-line plug into the plastic, skate away and maybe start moon-walking or even pull out the heavyweight-belt celly. Let the scouties and the rockets know you're the best player out there. It's a prime time for cellys.

Cellys are perfect at other times in a game, too. Celly hard after you scrap, whether you win or lose. That's a big move dropping the mitts, so take the moment. A celly after taking a penalty is a great way to fire up the crowd. Flooding the scoresheet is key, but don't forget to celly the little things, too: blocking bisccies for the rockets, running numbies on a rookie four feet from the boards, slew footing a tendy who's dumb enough to challenge you for the puck behind the net. All great plays, all deserving a sweet celly. Here are a few more celly-worthy moments:

- Celly in the penalty box.
- Celly during the national anthem.
- Celly in the locker room before the game.
- Celly after missing an open net.

- Celly on the bench after every goal, every hit, every whistle, every shift, every time out.

Pretty much celly any chance you get. Remember, beauties celly.

TOP 5 CELLYS

1. **_The Punt:_** A partner celly and easily one of the best that we have. It's simple, yet more challenging than it looks. This one will really help you stand out with the scouties.
2. **_The Harpoon:_** A classic solo celly. Use it often.
3. **_Standard Sword Swipe:_** This one lets everyone know you have class, but a touch of flash, too.
4. **_Flag Pole:_** Ever tried to toss out a flag pole? This is only for the masters of cellys.
5. **_The Line Dance:_** There's nothing better than clickin' heels with a teamie for a line dance celly.

BACK-CHECKING

This term doesn't really fall into our vocabulary. People talk about back-checking all the time, but to us it sounds like way too much work. You will burn your energy up too quickly if you are getting back as fast as possible. Plus, you take away your chance of sniping that greasy b-way twine tickler. In short, back-checking is for coach's pets, so you probably don't want to do that.

CHUCKIN' SAUCE

The best way to pass the puck is to send some UFOs across the ice. Every time you are trying to dish the bisccy, get it as elevated as possible. Unnecessary sauce is always necessary, don't ever forget that.

Most people think that sauce is all about moving the puck heel-to-toe on your twig. That's wrong. As soon as you open your twig up like that, everyone knows exactly what you're about to do and they will try to pick it out of the air. You have to be able to sneak through your sweet-and-sour sauce. So, toe-to-heel is the only way. No one will ever know it's about to happen because it never looks like you're ready to send some pizzas through the air. It will also make the bisccy flutter, which is what you want. A flat bisccy may look pretty, but a fluttering one will bounce over twigs if it lands short of the targgy. If it takes a hop over the targgy, too, that's no problem. It'll give your teamie something to skate into and wheel down the ice.

GREASIN' YOUR TIP

When you're in front of the pipes making the tendy smell what you had for lunch, you want to always try to grease your tip. Getting your wood on the rubber after a ripper from the point is key. Screening the tendy is a great idea, but stealing that snizz from a teammate is even better.

Tipping the bisccy past the pipes is going to take a lot of work and praccy. The easiest and most effective way to grease your tip is by facing the shooter. Seeing where the puck is coming from is going to make it a lot easier to get your wood on it. Opening your blade up is going to help you control where it goes. Whether you want it high or low, you can get either with an open blade.

If you have a mid-cheese missy coming in hot and you know the tendy is floating like a butterfly, point the tip of your blade toward the top corns that you want to pick and let the bisccy hit the heel and roll right up where Momma keeps the peanut butter.

If the tendy is playing more of a stand-up game, then you want to try for low cheese. Point the tip of your blade toward the shooter and now the heel of your twig is pointing at whichever bottom corner you want. The bisccy is going to hit closer to the toe and roll off the heel. If you have the right T.J., the puck will actually pick up speed as it comes off your twig, and the tendy will have no chance stopping it.

If there's a heater coming along the ice at you in front of the net, then you really only have one option. Keep your twig pressed hard on the ice and open that blade way up like a butter knife. If you do it right, when the puck hits your twig, it's going straight up. Playing pipe music when you're greasin' up your tip is some of the most beautiful music ever.

There are only a few players that might be able to perform some of these more advanced tips. Don't beat yourself up if you can't get the hang of them. No one is as good as we are, so you can't expect to be able to do what we do.

The b-hand tip is a tough one. For this tippie, you're looking for more of a full scoop and going top corns every time, or at least right into the tendy's cheeseburger chomper. Get your shouldies perpendicular to the shooter, so you can see where the bisccy is coming from and where you want to put it. As the puck gets to you, start with your twig a few inches lower than it, and scoop it up and launch it as hard as you can. This will almost always put it top corns—and if it doesn't go in, then you're giving a fan a souvenir. Again, the most important thing about tipping shots is making sure someone else isn't getting your snizz. Whether you score or not doesn't matter, as long as no one else scores either.

If you want a real challenge, then you are going to want to try the speed burst tip. Get your back to the shooter, and with your head on a swivel, watch for it coming in. Have your twig cocked and locked in clapper position, and when the bisccy gets in range, swing for the fences. A full connection of the bisccy is going to increase the speed of it by a minimum 50 mph. Even if you end up hitting the tendy right in the chest—with power like that, he isn't going to be able to breathe for the rest of the night.

Probably the most dangerous and lethal tip is the c-check tip. It sounds straightforward, but it will take years of praccy to even pull one off. Get your back right against the tendy, so he has to stand up to see around you. You are looking for mid-cheese missies for this tip. Keep your twig just above your belly button, and do not lose sight of the puck. When it's right there for a tip, cross-check straight down and bounce the bisccy in the five hole. It works 100 percent of the time when you make contact. It also hurts 100 percent of the time when you don't make contact.

The hardest one of all is the tip to one-tee. This tip takes the most amount of skill. When you're posted up in front, you want to knock the puck down to your feet and in one swing take a quick one timer. Even pulling off this one once is highly unlikely. If you happen to, though, you better make sure someone got it on film or no one is ever going to believe you.

Whichever tip you're going for, if you want to work on keeping them good and greasy, then there are a few different drills you can do. First, go to your local batting cages. Kind of like Happy Gilmore did, but instead of taking the heaters to the chest, grab your 5030 and try to deflect the balls toward all the other people in the cages. If you don't have any batting cages near you, then go to your local dollar store or anywhere that sells bouncy balls and buy around 100 of them. Find a room big enough that you can swing your twig all around. Now make a pile of all the bouncy balls and, when you are ready, take the hardest clapper you can to send them all flying. As the balls are whipping around the room, start tipping them and changing the directions of each ball. It works perfectly. Give it a try and tag us in the videos, so we can see the progress.

CHIRPS, BEAKS, AND TRASH TALK

Any good hockey player can chirp, or beak, or trash talk. What's the difference? Absolutely nothing. The fact that you didn't know that is comical, and a great reminder of your dire need for the fundies. All these terms basically mean making fun of an opponent, or even your own teammate. But during game-play, try to focus on the dumbbells you're playing against.

All good chirps are original. You can't use the same beak over and over again—you'll just sound like one of those annoying parakeets at the pet store, and it won't have the same effect. You also want it to be quick. No one cares if you write a mean essay, so get to the point, skeeter.

It's tough to think up new creative chirps on the fly, so a great way to start chirping is to compare whoever it is to an inanimate object. Anything from "you squid" to "you look like a baby carrot." They really don't make any sense, and that's the point: it'll throw them off guard because they won't understand the comparison. As an added bonus, when they ask their buddies what these chirps mean, one of them might stick and become an unwanted nickname.

Being good at chirping is going to take years of praccy. It isn't for everyone. Some people just aren't cut out to toss around some daggers and get in some heads. But if you try, and work at it every day, you can come up with some solid chirps as you make your way through the ranks.

DEALING WITH COACH

No matter what, you are always going to have a coach. You can't have a hockey team without a coach. It's some weird rule that doesn't make any sense because they don't actually do anything. Since they have to be there, though, you need to know how to deal with them.

The easiest thing to do is ignore them. Whenever they have something to say, just try to tune them out. If they are getting right up in your grill and you can smell all the onions they put on their sub, then we have a very special trick for you. It's time for a big sneeze. It doesn't have to be a real one.

Just get a big one coming out of your snot box and hit 'em with a quick head butt, so they stop getting after you. It works every time and has a very low percentage for getting a suspension.

PRESS BOX

There are two reasons why you would be in the press box. Either you are a healthy scratch or you are injured. If you've been paying attention to the fundies, then you should never be scratched and you should be the one out there sending plugs onto the I.R. But we can't hold your hand through this. Regardless, when you aren't at battle with the team, you have one job. Get the biggest basket of chicken fingies the arena has. The game doesn't matter since you aren't playing. So unless you're bored, you don't have to worry about watching it. The rest of the team is going to tell you all about it afterwards anyway, so grease a bucket of fingies and scope out the rockets in the crowd.

WARMIES AND BURNIN' WHEELS

Execution of the fundies is essentially useless unless there's a scoutie in the stands. So, in warmies, the first thing you wanna look for when you jump on the sheet is the scouties. Once you spot one in the stand, you really wanna amp it up. This is your moment. It's pretty much a show-and-tell to let the scouties and rockets in the bleachies see your greasy flow.

The only time you wanna burn wheels in warmies is when you run out of the gate. You want three or four full-speed laps, boys. Treat 'em like it's an all-star game. Once you've proved your speed, continue your warmies. Or, better yet, take a sit and save yourself for the game.

Never participate in the drills, boys. This just makes you blend in, and you don't want that. Plus doing all those drills will drain you for the big game. After you take some laps at full throttle (with the bucket off for maximum flow), grab six or so pucks, find a place in the middle of the blue line, and start stickhandling. Do this the whole warmy to really stand out.

You can also use warmies as a prime opportunity to get under your opponents' skin. When skating laps by centre ice, try stealing the pucks. This really

gets the boys going. Four to five laps of red line stealing is key. Once you've attempted to steal all their pucks, they will ask for them back. This is your time to shine. Start blasting clappers into their zone. Send 'em right at the tendy during a drill— you gotta let 'em know you're still here.

Make sure you're the first person on the ice for warmies and the first one off. This lets Coach know that you're ready to play. After that final buzzy ending warmies, you wanna skate as fast as you can to leave the ice. Let the crowd see your speed.

PRACCY

The fundies take time to learn, and you're going to want to praccy everything we're teaching you. But here we're talking about team praccy, boys. As natural athletes, we don't have to praccy at all. At best, we're hitting a fresh sheet just to dust iron a few times, maybe get a couple tillies going, or just rattle Coach 'cause we know more than any clipboard carrier out there. Since you aren't on our level, though, we'll touch base on it. But honestly, if you think that team praccy is crucial to getting better, then you probably also think that football takes real talent.

When heading to praccy, don't worry about being early. Give yourself just enough time to get onto the ice. The first five minutes of praccy never matter, so it's more like a buffer zone for you to get out there. When you hit the sheet, start twisting twig and burn a few bisccies off the glass. You want to hear how hard you're shooting, so don't stop until you get the sound you want.

One of the most important things during praccy is to always rip rubber on net when you're waiting to run drills. A lot of drills start from the corns, giving you ample opportunity to thread the needle off the far pipe. Tendies hate this 'cause they usually get hurt from rogue biscuits hitting the back of the legs, side of the dome, or even right in the back of the cranium. Don't worry about them; you don't need a tendy anyway. Like we always say, it's the easiest position. Your shooting is more important than the tendy's praccy, so keep busting them.

Every paper-cut coach always says, "Practise like you play." That is wrong. Never practise like you play, boys. That's how you waste energy. You don't want to burn yourself out before games or if you're going out that night, so burn hoof at maximum 50 percent. We call it the "max50 rule." That may be the most important fundy to remember about praccy.

If you know it's a no-puck praccy, then for sure you aren't going. Praccy is supposed to develop you. How are you going to get better without biscuits to rip?

Apparently, scraps in praccy are frowned upon. We disagree. If you want to be good at flipping finger pillows and speed baggin' booger bags, then you bet your 5030 assets that you better be yard sailing and massaging faces. Pick the newest guy on the team and get a couple uppies in on him. Don't dust him up like you would in a real game —we don't want to hurt anyone. But get in some body shots. It's crucie to stay on top of your game.

Outside of that, praccy isn't really good for much. Playing games is more important—but if you have nothing better to do, then praccy isn't a bad alternative. At least you're out greasin' steel on a fresh sheet. And worst case, just leave early—it's your time, so come and go as you please, boys.

GREASIN' THE INNY (INTERVIEW)

A huge part of being a beauty is demolishing an in-game interview. It isn't an everyday opportunity, so you have to capitalize whenever you get one. When speaking with a three-piece suit holding a mic, the most important thing that everyone forgets is to pump your own tires. We all know it's a team game. That's cool, talk about the boys and how special they are. But get to the point, and tell the fans what they want to hear.

Mention how sick your hands are and about that play in the first period where you broke four ankles with absolute rippers, then made a deadly toe-drag around the last pylon, before playing pipe music going c-bar and out. Make up an excuse for why you didn't snipe that top corns. Say that you just love the sound of classical pipe music. Talk about how much more ice time you deserve because you're so good. If you don't have confidence in yourself, then no one else will. Pump the tires nice and full, and keep talking until you get cut off at the end of the inny.

POST-GAME

When you come off the ice, you can choose to be either speedy or slow. If you like to get out quick, then hit the showers as fast as possible and get to the lobby for some fresh chicken fingies—maybe see where the rocket squad is. Don't waste any time if this is what you want to be. And don't bother stopping to hear what Coach has to say. He's just going to say the same thing he always does (whatever that is), so don't worry about it.

Now, if you're taking your time, then it's all about the stories—your stories, not whatever Coach is saying. This is when you want to tell everyone about how great you played. Talk about when you steamrolled the tendy, taking the bisccy hard in the paint. List all the PIMs you got before going into all the reasons why you didn't snizz today, and who messed up your chances for some apples. Remember that the last players out always have to look like they were trying to hurry: leave your shirt unbuttoned halfway with an absolutely atrocious half tuck, with your unknotted tie hanging around your neck. Walk out of that room and through the lobby like you own it.

6 POSITIONS

DEFENCE: BREAD AND BUTTER, HEART AND SOUL, REAL FAMILY-TYPE GUYS

The title says it all. Forwards can win you a game, but defence will win you a championship. A solid D-man is always thinking and always moving. On average, they think five seconds faster than any other position. This means they can see when a passing or shooting lane is going to open and send the biscy for a ride with deadly accuracy and ease. The first outlet pass is how you know if you have a good D-man. Tape-to-tape passes across the ice, threaded through the entire team in front of you, are an art only a D-man can master. It is one of the most majestically underrated plays in the game.

With only six or seven D-men on a team, and two at most on the ice, they work the hardest. Even when they aren't skating, they aren't being lazy. They are conserving and monitoring and attacking before you even know it's happening. It's all strategy. It's a thinking game on the back end. That's why they win the championships. If the other squad's forwards can't get past your defence to score, then your forwards shouldn't have to score as many goals.

FORWARD: THE PLAYERS THAT GET ALL THE CREDIT THEY DON'T DESERVE

Everyone can agree that forwards get too much credit. You don't agree? That's fine, lots of people have terrible opinions all the time. Think about it. In five-on-five game-play, the majority of the players are forwards, so yeah, statistically speaking, they should score the most goals. We're not saying they're not necessary—without forwards the game wouldn't work. And they do bring a lot of energy and tempo to the game. They also give the D-men someone to pass to.

There are three forward positions: two wingers, one on the left and one on the right, and in between those boys is the centreman. The centre's job is to win all the face-offs and basically cover every part of the ice. As centreman, you have to support your D-men and then also be hard into the offensive zone to spray the tendy with snow.

You don't actually have to support the D-men, though. If you want to get the most goals, then it's best to always play high. Don't come any lower than your bluey; ideally, you want to be floating around the centre line. Don't move around too much, though. Save your energy for when the puck squirts out and then switch gears to speed burst. There can only be one cherry picker, so if a winger gets it first, then you're floating bluey.

Wingers, you have it pretty easy. All you need to know is what side you play. When you figure out your side, stay there and get out of the way of anyone going for an end-to-end rush. For the rest of the time, get open so the defence can pass you the puck, and then immediately pass to your centre. The centre is always the best forward, so give him the puck. You are basically there to set up the centre and be a garbage goal kind of guy. It's super simple, and if we say too much more, you will probably get confused.

TENDY

We have always said it: tendy is the easiest position in the game. Think about it. There's usually only two on the team, and only one generally plays an entire game. If it were difficult, they would have a line of tendies changing on the fly just like the rest of the boys. Still, we get asked all the time to show some fundies for the tendies, so we have adapted our thinking to incorporate them. As easy as it is, there are some key fundies. Most are common sense and we shouldn't have to go too heavy into those. But letting dust bags rip rubber missiles at you is super weird, so where's the common sense in that?

Your crease is your safe place and should be dangerous territory for anyone else, zebras included. Protect the paint, own the paint. You can't get hit when you're there, and if you do, then it's go time. You have a wood plank on your hand that works perfect as a face massager. Don't be afraid to use it. Outside of the paint, you're fair game, though. Too often we see a tendy leave to play the puck and receive a little slew foot action and then lose it. Well, you earned it. You have to stick up for yourself, and if you want to stray out into the war zone, be prepared to battle. It's super crucial for you tendies to toughen up, toss your meat around, and keep it interesting.

Cellys need to be a part of your game. Shutouts don't happen often, so that's the absolute most perfect time to celly hard and cut the other team down. Don't just pump your fist either. Get creative and use your imagination. Throw down the Turtle Shell celly, where you spin on your back. If it was a real big game, don't just take the bisccy with you—grab the net. You earned it, so take it—and get your dad to toss it on the roof of the Caravan for you.

If you are sitting as the back-up tendy for the game, you got the even easier job. Even if you're bored, don't open the gate for plugs. If you end up having to go in and bail out your team, you don't want a strained chicken wing from constantly opening the gate. Instead, what you want to do is take your phone with you on the bench. Then you can listen to your music, send a few snaps here and there, and maybe get some fresh chicken fingies delivered to you if you're hungry.

The only save you want to make is a glove save. Why, you ask? Because it looks the coolest, why else? Don't ask dumb questions—you're trying to look flashy and get noticed. Blocker saves aren't flashy. A perfectly executed glove save should be a full windmill. You have to sell it, so everyone knows that you made the save and you can get a quick whistle. When you're protecting the pipes, it's a great idea to play heavy on your blocker side, meaning you keep that side of your body tight to that post, leaving ample room on your glove-hand side for the shooters. This will get them shooting where you want, which means you will be able to flip that popsicle stick you call an arm around nice and speedy and get the glove save every time.

If you get shots rippin' toward your chopping board (which is your blocker, meathead), then you can't really sell a big windmill. But if it happens, the main fundy for getting the biscuits off the pizza box is to always throw your chicken wing forward and really punch that biscuit. This will get it as far away from your pipes as possible, and that's really the whole goal of being a tendy. Try not to use the blocker, though. They don't look nearly as cool as a glove save, boys.

The last save style we want to take a look at is stacking the pillows. Think of your mom's couch on Christmas Eve when you're expecting company, so you have to have all the nice pillows out, stacked to the moon, so that no one can actually use the couch because those are the nice pillows and arranged perfectly. That's how we want your pillows stacked in the paint.

These are the only real saves that tendies make. Obviously, glove saves and pillow stacking are the most important because they get you on the highlight reel and they get the rockets looking your way. We know you're going to ask something ridiculous like, "If we're supposed to only glove save, then why do we need to know how to stack the tombstones?" The answer is simple. When a full bend is picking cherries and gets sprung on a lucky puck into a b-way, stacking the pillows is going to look absolutely deadly. And you're always stacking with the blocker side on the ice, so you have the glove up, ready for windmilling. Also, stacking up on plugs burnin' hoof on b-ways gives you a great opportunity to send 'em flipping over you. So by stacking the pillows, you can get a solid triple-triple: first the style points, second the flashy save, and third a well-served front flip to a pigeon. Picture it—that looks cool, and scouties want the cool kids.

The last thing to consider is what style of tendy you are going to be. There are two to pick from: the old-school stand-up like Ron Hextall, and the new-school butterfly like Marc-André "Flower" Fleury. Both have their perks. Being a stand-up tendy isn't really heard of anymore, so if that's you, then you will stand out. That's crucial as having the attention on you is exactly what you want. Upright tendies can kick-save, which works well for getting the bisccy all the way out of your zone. You can't do that in the butterfly. The best you can do is whip a G-save full windmill and drop the bisccy back in play if you have good enough defence. The best part of being a stand-up tendy is you don't get as tired. Going up and down all the time wastes so much energy.

Butterfly looks just ever greasy, though. Having those fresh pillows flat on the ice saying, "Nope not going low, buster." This gets them shooting high and, if you remember (we *just* went over this), we want to see all glove saves. And being low a lot of the time lets you set your sights on the backs of knees in front of the net. Lock in and catch 'em with quick jabs that will make those guys spill to the ice, clearing your view. Just think about what we taught Fleury: clearing the front of the net any way possible. He is arguably the best at it since the eppie came out.

CAPPY

Captains are the most important people on the ice. As a cappy, you have the power to do pretty much anything you want. If you wanna toss down the finger pillows and start throwing bones, do it. When you're tired and wanna sit a few minutes in the sin bin, maybe wheel the rocket scorekeeper. It's your ice, your team.

Cappy is the biggest beaut on the ice, the one all the scouties will be watching. This is why you wanna wear the C, boys. For us, the roles of a cappy are pretty simple. First, complain to the ice piggy on every call against the boys, even if it's a clear penalty or you didn't even see the call. When rippin' on the ref, you wanna be aggressive and loud. Let him know you aren't happy—maybe even break a stick and toss it in his direction. This will make the ref think twice next time before pumping air into a whistle.

Another trick to get back at the ref if he's still handing out PIMs is to skate as fast as you can into the corner that he's in and blow a tire. Fall into him or lay him out—just do whatever you can to crash into him. After you get up, start yelling at him as if it's his fault that he got in the way.

For some reason, sometimes the refs don't appreciate you yelling at them, but how else are they to know they're making bad calls? Refs may give you a penalty for chirping them, but it's part of the game, boys. Now, you gotta start chirping even more. This could send you to the dressing room with a ten-minute major and a game misconduct, so be careful. You only want the misconduct if you're losing, boys. You know the golden rule: if you're down in the game, you wanna get out as fast as you can, so it's not your fault.

Just as crucial, boys, the cappy is the one in the room who has control of the music. When picking pre-game notes, you wanna play one song over and over 'til game time. "Thunderstruck" is a pretty greasy pre-game tune, and the louder the better. This will really fire up the boys!

A lot of people think the cappy has got to make speeches, but generally you wanna let the As handle this, boys—mainly because you need to save your energy and voice for chirping the ref and the other team. But if it's a big game, then you want to be the one talking. Let the boys know what you want and how you want it. Tell 'em who's going where and when. Also, if you're not happy with the coach's line-up, go ahead and change that up how you like it.

ASSISTANT CAPPY

Although your goal is to be the cappy, there are some good benefits of being the assistant cappy. Wearing the A, you aren't held to as high of a standard. You still have to lead the way, but you can also get away with a lot more. If anyone has a problem you don't feel like dealing with, just send them to the cappy or the clipboard carrier. If you want the boys to listen up in the dressing room, just yell—take the respect you deserve. You aren't

trying to earn it—you are taking it. Having a letter on your jersey allows you to do this. It kind of acts like a highlighter, giving the scouts something to see. It gives you chances to go end-to-end whenever you want to impress the scouties.

Being the assistant cappy gives you the opportunity to be the coach, too. Anytime that you don't like what the paper cut is saying, feel free to change it up. You know more about hockey; that's why you are still playing and he isn't. Having that A on your chest gives you free reign to do as you please, boys. If Coach wanted to control you, he wouldn't have sauced it on. So, when you run numbies in the terror zone (three feet from the boards) and fire up a ten min., you won't have to worry about missing a shift because you can pull a fast one on the ice piggies and get one of the busters on the bench to serve it for you.

The assistant cappy role is probably the greasiest. You get all the same perks as the cappy with no responsibility. Rockets will have their eyes on you just because you are a loose cannon. The clipboard carrier never knows what to expect, so you will probably get double-shifted every game. If you don't produce or become a liability, you can always make excuses and toss the blame on someone else. The easiest way to scoop the A is probably scrapping in main camps and try-outs. If you can't get someone to bite there, then within the first couple weeks of praccy get a solid scrap in and celly hard—win or lose. You'll have that A on your chest in no time.

CLIPBOARD CARRIER

It needs to be said again, boys: the most important thing to remember is that coaches don't really matter. But I guess if you are going to be the dressed-up paper cut, there are a few fundies for you to follow and perfect.

First thing you need before even thinking of firing up a half Windsor (we all know you won't be able to grease a double) is a solid justification as to why you aren't still playing, or never made it to the show. Coaches always have that career-ending injury story. That is the classic, boys! Don't even try to stand behind the bench if you don't have yours nailed down. Smart play on their part—just don't fall for it.

Shoulders are always a good target. Tell those plugs how you used to hurt goalies from your blue line with a clapper sent from the heavens, but now you have trouble flippin' muffins to the moon 'cause the ol' chicken wing doesn't move like back in the day. *Do not* let the boys see you try to twist twig in praccy unless you have your story on point.

Another great targgy for an injury is a knee. Heck, double down on both knees from the same injury

and get yourself out of ever having to skate or train with the boys. Back in Jacob's prime, he was burnin' hoof through the middle, just crossin' the trolley tracks, tuckin' hip past some dust bags, when he caught the blue line. His pure speed mixed with a fresh sheet as the blue line claimed him, sending him straight into the boards, breaking just about every bit of his knees in one go. That is a perfect example of the type of story you need, and it's based on real life, so it makes it more believable.

Now that you have your career ender sorted out, the next big thing to think about is image.

Your main role is essentially to be a clipboard model. Get your hair cut, grease it back, look good. If you are up to the responsibility, and if you can handle the power that accompanies it, then you can bring in the greasiest mop chop known to man. Some have called it poetry for the dome, others consider it a lost art. It is the crown jewel for your melon. That's right: the mullet is a game-changer. In this position where image matters more than anything, the mullet will open any and every door for a bright future. Don't believe us? Then you should close this book and get back to doing your taxes or sorting your stamp collection.

As far as the team knows, you only have two outfits. Any days that are not game days, it's the team track suit, or tracky. Everyone believes you sleep in this—it's your pride and joy. Outside of the tracky, it's a suit. Never a tailored suit, though. Until you reach the show, you are rockin' one that's a little too small. This way when it's time to get fired up and the seams are feeling the stress, you might get a little rip going, giving you the opportunity to really tear it up with your bare hands.

Oh, and most importantly, keep a clipboard with you at all times—one that you know you can break for sure in one swing against your knee, the wall, a table, or your cappy's ugly mug.

Keeping up? Highly doubtful, but we're going to keep going anyway.

Next on the list: remember you are not there to be friends. Each and every conversation should be had in a tone that induces fear. Apparently, experts

say that people don't resp
respond to bonding expe
that, then you probably th
numbies four feet from the
leader, you need to be fea
looking mad is exactly wh
make it to the next level.

Outside of those key area
to coaching. Make sure yo
stats that you use as motiv
about. Pick a favourite on
that gets treated like he ca
garbage cans once a gam
Especially if it's a blow-ou
going into the second. The
going through a g-can! Ju
hard and turn those chees

COACH'S PET

This is short and sweet, boy
coach's pet. Don't be a coa
know what that is, then it's

7 RUBBER LAUNCHING

CLAPPER

This should be your most-used shot. If it isn't, then you probably shouldn't play puck. A good clapper is hard and high. Almost every coach is looking for a slapshot low and away from teammates, but that doesn't make sense. Head hunt, boys. If you want to be the one scoring the goals, then you need to clear out the traffic, and a low shot isn't going to do that for you. Nice and high will part those seas. If they don't move, then they'll probably hear their heart beating between their eyes.

To take a good clapper, you have to have the right grip on the wood. Naturally, your top hand is going to be on the knob. The bottom hand is going to be nice and low for maximum flex. Your bottom digit dialers should be about eight inches above the blade of your weapon. Grip it nice and tight: "grip it and rip it" is the name of the game, boys. Also, your melon better be buried, staring straight down at the biscuit that you are about to turn into a rubber ninja star. Keep your eyes down because if you don't know where you're shooting, then no one else knows either.

By using these tips and firing clappers as often as possible, you should increase your twine tickling by at least 2.78 percent.

WRISTIES

One of the deadliest ways to tickle twine is a wrist shot, or wristy. Everyone knows that you should always be taking clappers, but the wristy works when you need to switch it up to catch a tendy off guard. The best time to use a wristy is when there is no one between you and the net. Don't forget to bury your melon. One of the most forgotten wristy rules is if you don't know where the puck is going, then no one else does either. In fact, that is super crucial whenever you are taking any sort of shot.

The key to getting off a good wristy is to get a nice wide grip on your rubber launcher. Your bottom hand should be just above the blade to allow for maximum whip of the twig. Start with the bisccy as far back as possible. This shot is intended to take

time, so you want a long drag from behind your body, with the release well in front of you. The whole shot should occur over about eight seconds. In game-play that's a long time, so plan it well. When you are completing a good wristy, you never want to roll your wrists over. Keep them nice and loose and make sure the blade of your twig stays open, so you can send the bisccy to the moon.

It isn't a powerful shot, but it is a great way to snizz top corns or mid-cheese.

B-HANDS

The backhand shot is not for everyone. Never forget that, and don't get too cocky about a b-hand 'cause you probably aren't very good at them. Before we talk about a good b-hand bar burner, let's talk about the type of player that should never try them.

Too often we see people stepping out of their skill boundary and attempting to get fancy. If you sound like you're chopping down the entire rainforest when you stickhandle, then you should never let the bisccy leave your T.J. from the backside. And if your ankles look like a couple of marshmallows wrapped in bungee cords, this is not your shot. Trying to keep them sturdy is a great idea, but just because you increased your ankle flex from 48 to 95 does not grant you any more skill. On the same note, if your skate laces are stiffer than your ankles, you should get some new wheels before you even try to work on your hands.

A b-hand snipe starts with a fresh T.J. It doesn't matter which T.J. you pick, but it has to look fresh. The tape better be so nice that your twig looks like a Christmas present. After that comes the technique, which is what makes it difficult. When you are taking the shot, you always want to lean your body weight into the rubber. Your grip is nice and wide on your twig (not quite as wide as a wristy, though). The general motion of a b-hand is similar to shovelling. Hands start nice and wide and, as you grease the wheels up and as you get your twig up high, slide your hands closer together, ending full swing with mitts together and a full extension over your shoulder. The whole point of a backhand is to hit the bar train. If you aren't playing pipe music on a b-hand, then give the goal to someone else. You only want the ones that sound and look good.

Still unsure of who should be sniping b-hand? That's simple—players like us can snipe b-hand at will. Players like you probably do not snipe often, and that's why you're reading this book. If by the end you have taken it seriously and practised the fundies, then maybe you will get a few lucky backhands going, but it will take time.

The best way to praccy your backhand is to go to your mom's house and set up around 850 pucks in the driveway. Scoop those biscuits as high as you can, and try to put them in the backyard. This method is super effective because if you hit the house even one time, your mom is going to whoop your backside.

SNAPPIE

A quick snappie is probably the easiest shot to take. The quick release of a snappie accounts for maximum snizzing. It's another top corns shot. Really, every kind of shot you take, you should always try for top corns. A snappie is a mix of the wristy and clapper. You want to use it in tight spots where you have to shoot quickly. Or, if you are in a drought, getting a snappie off will increase your snizzing significantly.

The key to this type of twig twisting is to take the shot at full speed. Keep the toe of your stick on the ice and bring the heel of the blade up and behind the bisccy. Your mitts should be about shoulder width apart to get max flex on your wood. Whip the wrists down, pulling the heel of your twig down fast. When the heel contacts the ice, your twig will flex hard and fast, causing the puck to rip off your twig. More than likely it'll be tickling twine.

A lot of people struggle with a good snappie. Like all the fundies, it takes time to develop. Typically, if you want to get a nice greasy snapper like ours, you need to spend time rippin' biscuits—somewhere between 50 and 700 biscuits a day. Still, don't expect to hit our level. The simple fact is we were born natural athies and you weren't.

B-WAY OR PENALTY SHOT

Any true chel sniper knows how to snizz on a b-way or penalty shot. If you don't know what the difference is, then we really don't know how you've made it this far into the book. To make it easy on you, we're going to just refer to it as b-way.

Now, it should be one of your goals to get on as many b-ways as possible. The easiest way to do this is to cherry-pick—hang out at the far bluey, behind the other team's defence, and wait for a stray biscuit to come your way. As soon as you have it on your fresh T.J., get those wheels going and start burnin' hoof straight for the tendy. You have to be able to make game-changing decisions in the blink of a broken twig. That means "fast" for all you Gary Googles trying to search for the meaning right now.

So what shot do you pick? Are you dangling or sniping? Should you blow a tire and take out the tendy, then drive home the low-cheese missy? Or should you bury your melon and wheel straight through the tendy with the biscuit, all at once?

All of these are great plays. You need to think about your status when picking what to do. If you are in a drought and haven't hit the scoresheet in a while, then we would say to take a page out of Olly's book and go through the tendy. Next time you have a clear-cut b-way with no one close on your heels, skate right through the tendy—pretty much just walking the puck in for a quick snizz.

Now, if you have a back-checker on you trying to haul you down, then blow a tire for sure and run that tendy. This way you can draw a penalty, maybe tuck in a low-cheese greaser, and possibly force out the back-up tendy. If you can get all of that in one go, you've just got the ol' b-way three-fer. Nice job, boys.

Dangles and snipes are for the top corns hunters. The Great One always said something like,

"Shooter's shoot, apples are for the fourth line." When you're pickin' cherries and get that ripe one up the middle, start the dangles early. The scouties want to see flash. Make your name bar stick out. Toss in some leggies, a couple spinnies, and point to some rockets in the crowd and fire a wink. After you showboat awhile, let one buck— tuck the back knee and send a greasy snapper to the moon, playing that sweet pipe music as you snizz a hot one.

Even with these moves, there's no guarantee you'll score. You're not us. So the most important thing to remember about b-ways is this: if you don't score, fake an injury or break your twig. There has to be a reason that you didn't snipe. For the injury, your best option is to lose an edge and hit the end boards at full speed. Or, for the old failed twig move, flex your stick as hard as you can and break it in half, showing everyone in the rocket recliners that there was an obvious problem with your rubber launcher. Maybe toss what's left of it at the quippy manager.

GREASY SNAPPER (OLLY'S FAVOURITE SHOT)

My favourite shot is the snapshot. It's the best suited to my style of play. When you're as fast as me, burning wall, you don't have time to load up and send a clapper at the tendy's dome, so you have to be able to release a quick snappie in stride. This shot always catches the tendy off guard. It's one of the hardest shots to stop.

One of my other deadly shots is the backhand—a.k.a. the "backy." This is most useful when you're in the paint and in tight areas, but I'm able to elevate the backy top corns a foot away from the tendy.

ROUND-THE-WORLD GOALIE KILLER (JACOB'S FAVOURITE SHOT)

Think you're ready for some advanced training? You're wrong, but the deadliest shot ever—and my absolute favourite—has to be my special clapper: the round-the-world goalie killer. No one else has that shot in their bag, making me a stand-out for the scouties.

Boys, I really shouldn't be telling you about my spechy shot, but since I know that no one else will ever perfect it, I don't see why I can't. The general idea of the shot is maximum wind-up, making for maximum twig twisting, which in turn makes for maximum rocket launching, resulting in maximum twine tickling. This slapshot variation could potentially do fatal harm to a tendy if he happens to get in the way. Same goes for players. Once they see you winding up, they will part like a fresh comb-over on Kelly Hrudey.

If you're brave enough to try it, I'll walk you through how it's done. The most crucie part of the shot is to always start in front of the puck. This does two things. First, it hides the puck. You can even toss in a fake pass or shot and then cover it up quick to prepare for destruction. Second, it ensures that you have maximum wind-up. Starting behind the puck does not allow for correct wind-up—that's just a standard clapper. But when you start in front of the biscey, you ensure a full 'stension on your rocket launcher. Make sure your bottom chicken wing is fully extended at this point. If you break your bow here, you will miss out on the maximum flex part of the shot, so keep her stiff like Coach Tort's upper lip (John Tortorella, obviously).

As you raise the stick forward and then up, at the top of the swing start leaning into your shot. At this point, you have already increased your shot speed by at least 25 mph compared to standard clappies. The sheer speed of your face massagers coming around will start twig flex early, normally around the time when they are about waist high. This is called the "preh-load." That's French for super hard. With the stick swinging all the way around to come behind the puck, now it's time for contact with the bisccy. Lean back hard and pull that top hand fast to the moon as you push the bottom hand to the ice, getting a full flex on the 5030 that would make Robin Hood proud. After you roast toast on the bisccy, just let your weapon do what it wants. It will slow itself down and go where it wishes—don't try to chain 'er down, boys.

That is the best way I can grease you through how to take the shot without actually showing you. The key elly to remember is the whole shot occurs in less than two seconds when completed correctly. It'll take years of praccy to get halfway to my skill, but that's because I invented it, and I'm a lot better than you.

Like I said, you do not want to get in the way of the round-the-world goalie killer. But blocking shots is part of the game, so let's talk biscuit blocking.

BLOCKING BISCCIES

Generally speaking, blocking biscuits is a thing for coach's pets. There are some circumstances, though, where you're going to want to be fearless, get low, and make yourself big. When you have a couple rockets in the crowd, it's a perfect time to get in front of some rubber and show them how tough you are. There are hundreds of ways to block shots, and each can be just as effective as the next.

The flamingo is one of the best ways. Get one foot up behind you and coast on the other one toward the shot. This minimizes the chance of getting hit with a ripper while proving that you are prepared

to stand in front of one. The shooter was just able to get it around your rudders.

Another great method is getting nice and low with as wide a stance as possible. This leaves plenty of room for shots on the ice to get through, but your tendy should not have a problem saving those. If the shot gets up a bit, you'll catch it in the bread basket and be able to drop it in front of you to head down the ice for a chance at tickling twine.

Typically when you get down in front of bisccies, you want to go wheels first. Even though you aren't that pretty, you still don't want to take a frozen puck in the jiblets. The standard meat slide is probably the most common way to block a shot. With some speed, lie flat on the ice, make yourself long, and take away the low shot. The main reason to use this method is because you are hoping the shot will get lifted and not actually hit you. It shows everyone that you are willing to make the sacrifice, and if it doesn't hit you no one can get mad because you tried. Always slide into the shooting lane with your feet first and face the shot, so you can clearly see how bad it's going to hurt. If you are lucky, it will hit you in the shin pads. If the shooter is smarter than you and hesitates, it's going to hit you right in the chest. Prepare yourself for impact and enjoy that last breath of air for the next five minutes. You'll sound like you're sucking slew water as you try to get air back into your lungs.

If you end up going face first into a shot block, get your chin right down on the ice and your finger pillows up in front of your face. If it's going to hit you, it's going to hurt you. There is, however, a huge bonus to these shot blocks. Any rocket in the stands is going to have sympathy for you if you get hit, and if you don't, they're going to think you are brave. That's a good card to play on a Friday night!

If you are actually trying to stop the puck, the one knee tuck is a solid block. Make yourself big and get down on one knee. Turn your body sideways and get your chicken wings out. This makes you as big as possible and the chances of the puck hitting you are pretty high. Also, the chances of you getting up and wheelin' on a b-way are pretty low. You need to decide if you want the goal or the assist if you are going to block bisccies.

8 QUALITIES OF NATURAL ATHLETES LIKE OLLY AND JACOB

COMPLETE PACKAGE

OLLY

You'll notice I'm a certified beauty when I run out of the tunnel for warmies. My speed makes me an absolute weapon, and I'm a tendy terminator with a release that should be illegal. Not only do I have the hardest shot on the ice, but I'm also blessed with the best flow in hockey—pretty much a complete package. Burning wall, greasin' brake peddy at the hashies, maybe firing it low cheese —who knows! I could come around the basket and hit the tendy with a quick wrappy. My arsenal is endless, my skill is limitless, and my power is unmatched. Some people say I'm a god at hockey. I just say I AM hockey.

JACOB

One of my best qualities is my natural-born ability to twist twig and rip rockets. I've got the most powerful shot that I have ever seen, and many others agree. And the pure speed that blazes off the wheels has to be second-to-none. I'm pretty sure I melt the ice with every stride.

LEADERSHIP

OLLY

When it comes to leadership, boys, that's where I flourish. I've always been the cappy on any sports team I've ever played for, even soccer. As a kid, boys, I'd tape a C onto my jersey. Coach never liked that move, but I'm a beauty so I did it anyway. Here's a little fundies tip: if Coach gives someone else the cappy, do like I've done for the past 20 years, and just tape one on your jersey.

JACOB

Basically, every team that I have played on, I have been the captain. And the teams where I didn't get the C, I pumped some eyes shut until I got what I wanted. Gotta be a leader, boys.

TILLIES

OLLY

I can't really talk much about this, boys. I'm currently 0–64 when it comes to tossin' meathooks. Like the Great One once said, "You gotta lose a few before you win."

JACOB

When it comes to shedding the finger pillows, it's rumoured that I'm in my own weight class. Not because of my size, but because of my unmatched skill. Sending sledgehammers from the South Pole straight to the booger bag, folded five style. Southpaws don't stand a chance against the Alberta bow, a couple chicken wings coming in hot at the snot box. Oh and most importantly, I am the king of a fresh-served hippie, buckling knees since 1990. It's a great way to start a tilly.

PUCK CONTROL

OLLY

My approach to puck control is simple: dominate. Every time the puck's on my tape, it looks like a magic trick. My control is second-to-none. In most games, it looks like I have a string running from my stick to the puck. I can toe-drag anyone and deke past every player on the ice without effort. Don't get down on yourself if you aren't a puck prince like me. It took many hours of practice, which I did in Bangladesh.

JACOB

As probably the greasiest player to grace the game, there's no doubt that I know all the quintessentials of good puck domination. I don't just handle the biscuit, I butter it up, making it look nice and soft when I have my mitts on it. I can turn on a nickel, making it near impossible to get the puck from me. What most people forget is that it's not just about how you stickhandle, it's also about how you move on your wheels. My side steps, stutty steps, and crossies are unmatched. Meaning

I can move my body with the puck six feet in less than a second. So while you are trying to figure out where I slipped off to, I'm tickling the twine and already mid-celly. So basically, I'm the best.

9 THE LOCKER ROOM

This is where church begins. The sanctuary of the game, boys. You begin and end every skate here, so it's a huge part of being a good pucker. When it comes to fundies of the locker room, it's more like unsaid rules.

ROLES

There are many different types of locker room guys. We will try to grease you through the most important ones, but these are pre-programmed when we are born. It's just about recognizing where you fit.

PRANKER

Locker rooms can be full of pranks, and there is always at least one pranker. Leaving your gear unattended is dangerous. If you're the pranker, never take it too far, though. Keep it clean and subtle, just enough for a solid laugh. Unless you're dealing with a rock pile, then for sure take it too far and tape all their gear together nice and tight, so they miss warmies. Be warned: if you're tossin' out pranks and you aren't a vet on the team, you are in line to receive some serious revenge.

Keep your head on a swivel, boys. Just like playing defence—you gotta know what's around. To get a good prank going, it's best to work solo. Getting someone to help runs the risk of people finding out who did it. If your name is leaked, you'll end up the victim of sock tape on your skate blades. When you hit the ice, you'll look like Bambi, with even bendier ankles than you had before. Your parents didn't even know that was possible.

Always make sure you have a mean poker face. When your trap works, you can't look suspect. Enjoy the laugh but don't laugh prematurely. Keep in rhythm with everyone else. Play it cool, even act like you're going to help solve this absurd crime. You need to be both subtle and assertive. It isn't something that can be taught. Start small with your pranks, don't bite off more than you can chew, and work your way up.

AUDIO BOY

One of the most important people in the room is the audio boy. Pre-game in the meat cooler is about getting amped up. Light that fire in the room and get ready for the battle. The key component is obviously music and this beauty's in charge of it. There's a fine line for an audio boy: you can't play any slow songs or techno and once a song is played that the boys don't like, he's canned—that's it.

Find the biggest, loudest speaks you can and get a solid playlist going. Keep to the essentials: start with "Sandstorm." No words in the song means no one's going to attempt a hero singalong and ruin everything. Of course, mix in some good ol' rock and roll: AC/DC is a staple. If you don't have "Thunderstruck," "Back in Black," "Hells Bells," and "For Those About to Rock (We Salute You)" in that list, then please, kindly close this book and re-evaluate everything you stand for. Figure it out and then continue reading.

Get some new-school stuff in there, too, a nice mix of upbeat and fast paced. We want hearts pumping and adrenaline flowing. Pick one song you leave the room to every game, and put it on five minutes before hitting the ice. Olly would always make his team listen to "Untouched" by the Veronicas before every game. It's a solid singalong and gets you ready to go. Jacob was always more for "Something Like That" by Tim McGraw—you know, a real feel-good country song that brings the room to life. The beats are the most important part of getting amped up because we all know that every single coach is coming in to talk about something no one cares about to try to inspire you to play hard. Just tuck your head and suffer through it 'til you can crank the music back on. We know it's hard, but it's doable. Don't let Coach kill the buzz, boys.

THE HOTSHOT

There's only room for one of these guys in the locker room. The hotshot is the cool guy. Even if no one else thinks they're cool, hotshots always think they are the coolest, and always do whatever they can to be the centre of attention. The hotshot is always the last one dressed and on the ice, living by the fashionably late rule. These guys never like other people's jokes and always display a smirk like they have something better to say. And you can't forget they claim they're always ready to fight and can beat anyone up, yet they never drop the gloves with anyone, even as a joke.

ALSO WORTH MENTIONING

There are a lot of different types of players in the room, boys. You got the suitcase, somebody who can't stay on one team for very long and gets traded every year. On the other hand, you got the glue guy, somebody who plays on the fourth line and isn't very good, but is an absolute gem in the locker room. This is the kind of guy who brings all the boys together. Every team needs a glue guy.

The puck nerd is somebody who doesn't have a very good connection with the team. It's usually the best player. On bus trips, he's studying game tape, going over stats, and taking naps instead of wheelin' rockets on Instagram or watching classic movies.

And you have the chatterbox. This guy sits in his stall and talks about stuff nobody's interested in (usually a corner guy).

Obviously, one of the worst players on the team, boys, is the coach's pet. This plug blocks shots in practice, skates hard every single drill, takes 30 second shifts, and never gets a penalty. This is the kind of player you want to stay away from once you start talking—he's gonna run to Coach and tell him everything. It's a dangerous trap. One of the best ways to get along with a coach's pet is to talk about the next game and how you're gonna skate hard, get pucks deep, blah blah blah—you know, coach stuff.

Here's a few more that really shouldn't need explaining:

1. **Rock Pile:** a rookie.
2. **Plug:** fourth liner.
3. **Tape Bandit:** somebody who never has sock tape.
4. **Grocery Stick:** like the little plastic checkout divider when you're buying groceries, this useless guy mostly sits on the bench, separating the forwards and d-men.

There's a lot of different players in the room, and they all play an important role. Know your role on the team, boys.

THE SHRINE

The stall you pick is your shrine that day. If it's your home barn, then you're sitting in the same place every game. Your ritual and superstitions can be the make-or-break of any game. So every game, follow your regimen to a T when setting up your shrine. No one can tell you what your superstitions are, so we'll tell you about ours.

JACOB

When playing pro in the Virgin Islands Elite Hockey League, mine were pretty simple, boys. At my stall, I always spread all my gear out over the stall next to me. I always got Coach to stick a rock pile beside me, so I could take over his stall and send him to fill my water and heat my towel for my pre-game shower. Gotta have the flow looking super greasy for the buckyless warmies. Every game, that stall was beside the door to the ice. Givin' all the boys some knucks and being the last one on the ice was crucie to me. Those knucks were an attempt to give some of the other boys a little more skill—as a natural-born leader, it was my job to let them touch greatness. Super-simple rituals for me, boys. You don't need that many when you are born with this kind of skill.

OLLY

That's right, boys, pre-game setty is soups crucial. Mine was simple, too, boys. Playing in the Bangladesh Pro League, every game I would get there 45 minutes before warmies, even though I don't warm up. I liked to watch and scout the rocket recliners for scouties and potential first (and last) dates. This is the only reason to arrive early for warmies, boys. When I got to the room, I would always switch up the stalls and sit in the spot of whoever was racking up the points, messing with his mojo to get the spotlight back on me. Then I would sit and stare down everyone in the room, so they knew it was my room. Gear stays in the bag 'til I'm ready to get dressed. Five minutes before warmy is when I would get geared up. That's right, boys—always miss the first five minutes of warmy and get out just as the stands fill up. That's when I would start my second round of scouting. With 30 seconds left in warmies, I'd take a lap. Nice and wide, crossing the red line and chopping down some ankies, trying to start some scraps early. I was always the last one on the ice and I would fire 17 pucks into the other team's net before leaving. I found it was a great way to get an opening face-off scrap. Super-simple richie, boys.

SPEECHES

Pre-game speeches are always going to be hit and miss, boys. Our best advice for these is to get the ear buds in and just listen to your tunes (unless maestro is on his game). If cappy is flapping his beak, listen to what he has to say, but as soon as he goes over a minute and a half, tune him out. He's just trying to be a coach's pet now. It's best not to stress about the game anyway, and most likely the garbage cappy and coach are just going to talk about basics you already know. It's a much better idea to think more about what you'll be doing after the game, so you can stay loose. "Pump up" speeches generally suck, except for Jacob's—he gives a mean speech.

10 BEYOND THE ICE

GETTING RESPECT

Respect isn't something that you earn in hockey. Respect is something that you demand. If you are new to a team, you have to walk in and take the respect that you deserve. You aren't there to make friends—you're there to play puck. Stop shaking hands and asking how they're doing. Announce who you are and where you will be playing. Kick someone out of their stall and immediately tell everyone how good you are and why you are better than them. If you want to be taken seriously, step up and take that respect that is rightfully yours.

THE BIG CONNY

Signing that big contract is huge. Obviously, you followed the fundies and improved your game 1000 percent by following everything we have to say. First thing to do when you get that conny is send a thank-you note to us. After that, you have to celly hard. Go out with all the boys and treat yourself to a nice dinner at the Pizza Hut buffet. Then cap the night off with some chel.

OFF-SEASY: HITTING THE LINKS

You shouldn't have a very long off-season if your team is any good. You will, no doubt, have some sort of off-season, though. Either way, this is your time to just kick it. Don't worry about training or anything like that. You worked hard enough throughout the season. The best thing you can do is hit the links and smash some dimpies. Being a good golfer goes hand-in-hand with being good at puck. That's why we all golf. It's just like taking clappers. It's a super-easy sport.

THE GRAPE CHALLY

A lot of people say that Connor McDavid is the greatest player in the game. Without a doubt, he is a great player. When we were asked to challenge him and teach him some fundies, we had a lot of things that we wanted to go over. His shooting was at the top of the list, though. So to really test his skill, we made up the grape chally.

After watching some of McDavid's game footy, we noticed real quick that he didn't ever tuck his knee as low as he could to get max flex on the twig. His hands were held too close together, and his wrists always seemed to curl over. There was never any tension in his arms, and so he was losing power potential. It was a natural decision to focus on his shooting—and also eliminate any thought that he might be the best. People need to remember that we are the best hockey players ever, and the grape chally settled this.

Using dental floss, we strung grapes on the net, top corns. As you all know that's our favourite shot to grease and naturally super easy for us to snipe the targgies. Before we let McDavid onto the rink, we dusted somewhere between three and 7,000 grapes out of the top corns on both sides. We even gave ourselves a challenge and tossed in a couple mid-cheese missy shots. After we knew how easy it was to snipe the grapes, we let the little guy onto the rink to see what he could do.

With two fresh grapes laced up for him and a fresh twig, we let him fire away.

There's absolutely no doubt that we sniped better, with significantly more power and accuracy. Anyone who has seen the eppie knows that we won the chally. The kid was good, though, mostly lucky, but not too bad for a rookie. He was using one of the twigs that Olly was rippin' with and it was already warmed up, which made it easier to lock in on the grapes and tickle the corns.

It was a great first run of fundies for him, but he still needs a lot of work to bring his game up to speed. Since we're the two best coaches in the world, we're committed to giving him another chance.

SECRETS TO HAVING A LONG CAREER

One of the secrets to a long career in the league, boys, is to let everyone know you're the best. Constantly brag about your ice time. After every shift let everyone on the bench know you almost scored. The more you tell the boys and coaches about how you're the best player on the team, the more they believe it.

DRY SPELLS

If by chance you happen to have a bad shift—obviously very unlikely for us—but if this happens to you, there are moves you can pull to save face by transferring fault to the boys instead of owning it.

First move: blow a tire into the boards as soon as you touch the puck. Really sell it, boys. Pop your melon cover off, toss a glove, let 'em know you're hurt. Make sure the trainer comes out to help—that just adds to the magnitude of the injury.

Your next move will depend on the current score in the game. If your team is down, just leave the game. As the superstar of the team, you don't want the weight of this loss on your shoulders. If your team is winning, different story, boys! Head to the locker room for a few minutes. Fire off a few texts to let everyone know where the party is after the game, maybe take a selfie or two, and get back out on the bench. Let the boys know you're the toughest player. No one will give you grief for not snizzing this game, and the boys will be working hard to make sure you get a scoring chance.

The cardinal rule during a dry spell is to take creddy for every goal your team scores, in any way possible. If you're on the ice for a goal but didn't have anything to do with it, celly like you just tucked rubber. Glass jump like it's a game seven overtime goal. Even if you weren't on the ice, let the boys beside you and the coach know that you told that guy to shoot there or you told him to wait in that position. This is just building your creddy, boys.

11 BEING A PURE BEAUTY

After learning all the fundies here, you are now an elite player. Try not to let it go to your head. But the work isn't done and there are more fundies to learn. We have fundies for everything, boys.

O.D.R.—OUTDOOR RINK

The sacred ground of hockey. Where the game originated and where we take it back to its roots, every winter. The O.D.R. is the closest thing to heaven.

If you want to survive on the O.D.R., you need to know a couple things. The first thing is *sticks in the middle*. This is how you start a game of pick-up puck. Everyone tosses their twigs in the middle and then one person, usually the youngest or the rock pile of the group, starts grabbing twigs completely at random, with his eyes closed, and

tossing them onto two piles, which become your teams. When all sticks are divvied, it's go time!

The second thing you need to know: there are no rules. The O.D.R. is a free-for-all, and game-play is based on how aggressive people get. If you get some stray lumber against your rudder, take note and make sure that you get 'em back!

The O.D.R. is where Canadians are born. It's why we are naturally so good at puck. You won't beat us at our game on our sacred stomping grounds. If you do, then it's because we let you win. We are literally that nice that if we win too many times in a row, we will sit back and let other people win here and there. We need people to keep playing against us!

HOCKEY TALK

Hockey players as a whole have a completely different language from everyone else. Most of the time, an outsider has no idea what is being said or whether it's good or bad. That's part of the whole language, though. It's so we can chirp the rock piles out of the game and not have to square up and serve them some folded fives. Basically, hockey talk is a lot of abbreviations and adding an "ie" or "y" to the ends of the abbrevies. It's a really simple concept—but hard to catch on to if you aren't exposed to it daily like we are. At this point in the book, if you haven't figured this out, you're going to want to go back and reread everything.

NICKNAMES

An extension of hockey talk, nicknames are super easy. Take the last name (or, in rare cases, the first name) of a player and add the "ie" or "y" to it— boom, there's the nickname. Some players have different names they go by, but those are usually self-assigned nicknames and typically aren't beauties. There are exceptions, though.

Nicknames can describe anything from the style of play to how someone looks. "Stone hands" is a common one. This name accompanies players that sound like they are taking an axe to the ice as they stickhandle, always fumble the biscuit, and can't catch a pass to save their lives. If you are a fast skater, you might get called "speedy" or "wheels." If you're a little guy that likes to toss the meat around, a good nickname would be "rhino" or "wrecker." The possibilities are endless.

BUS TRIPS

Roadies are a huge part of playing puck, and bus rides are a super-crucial part of being a superstar. The first key to a roadie is getting the right seat. You want to show up a little early. If you are a vet on the team, you obviously aren't putting your bag on first. Leave it to the side and get the first rock pile you see to toss your meat covers in, so you can be first to grab your gear when you get off the bus. Everyone knows that the very back seats are reserved for the vets and the captains. If you are new to a team, that first year you aren't sitting any farther back than the middle. But make sure it's far enough back that you can't be seen as the coach's pet. If you even try to get back to the vets' seats, you can count yourself in for a trip to kangaroo court. No one wants to go there, but everyone wants someone to mess up and let the law take place. Choosing your seat is tricky, but you will figure it out.

Now that you have a seat, it's time to get started with basic roadie rules. First thing you need to know is always come prepared. Get a bunch of snacks and a tray of Timmies double-doubles if you want to make it the whole trip. If you are a rock pile on the team, make sure you have good movies: the classics like *Slap Shot* and *The Waterboy* are always good to keep in the arsenal. Never hesitate to toss in the movie, as it could save you later down the line. But don't seem too eager either. Vets are always looking for something to grease you up about.

Any and all food that is supplied by the team always starts at the back of the bus. Better keep your diggies off the subs unless you have some sort of seniority on the team. The beauty part of being a vet is you own that bus. Pick any seat you want, and even move rookies around how you like. You get to eat first—and if you don't like a movie, you can have a different one put on at any time.

Roadies are where you become a family. The bus is always where the best stories are told, and also where they stay. No matter what the outcome of a game, the trip home is never dull. Maybe a few post-game wobbly pops if you're of age, and always a few stories about who had who's back and who better keep their head up next time you play them. Then it's on to the next game. It's where all the most unreasonable strategies are drawn up, and they don't work 84 percent of the time. Roadies are one of the most important parts of the game. The bus is your second home, and in Olly's case, it's where he spent 92 percent of his away games as a healthy scratch.

HOCKEY MOMS

First and most importantly, hockey moms are heroes! They are a special type of mom and the most important factor in the life of a good hockey player. There aren't a whole lot of fundies to go over for hockey moms. That's the thing about moms—they are always at least one step ahead of you. Even if you think you are catching up to them, you aren't. Moms are crafty. They plan everything and will go ten miles extra to make sure it all goes smoothly.

Since this is the book of fundies, we will go over a few points. Then when the moms read it, we will adjust things according to what they tell us because they are always right. The first thing to go over is the snacks. Hockey moms always have snacks. Whether they made them or they got them somewhere, they always have the best snacks that you've never heard of until they whip them out of their purses—bags that seem to hold everything, including the shin pad you lost after the last game.

They always have everything ready to go and they always remember what you are going to forget before you have a chance to forget it. Make sure you always say thank you to your hockey mom for driving you through the worst snowstorms, for the 6 A.M. practice, or for getting you out of school early for a tourney. Tell your mom you love her, because if it weren't for our moms, we wouldn't be around to even think about playing puck!

HOCKEY DADS

A hockey dad is one of the most important elements for kids coming up, trying to get into the show. If you want your kid to be successful and make it to the next level, then you need to help. There are some super-crucial parts of being a hockey dad that can help get your son or daughter to that next part of their career.

The first—and possibly most important—fundy of being a hockey dad is to remember that even though you don't stand behind the bench with the team, you are the coach. You know more than the coach, and you will teach your kid everything they need to know. If you don't like how practices are being run, or you don't agree with the systems that the coach is using, then switch it up. Take your kid to the O.D.R. and show them what they should be doing. You aren't a fan of the 1-2-2 passive forecheck for protecting a lead? No one is, bud. So if you see that being used, get them thinking offence first. Teach them the blitz, or a 4-1 aggressive forecheck. The whole point of the game is to score more goals than the other team, so teach them to score as many as they can—a passive forecheck just isn't going to maximize snizzing. You may not agree with several things the coach is teaching, so every time you see something you don't like, make sure you work with your kid and teach them exactly what you want to see.

It's also an essential part of hockey dad fundies to prepare where and how you watch the games. First thing you want to do is get there early—this is what we call the "scope and scoop." Look around and find that best spot to stand. You want to be able to see the whole rink and be visible to all the parents on your team as well as the opposing team. Typically, we don't want to see you sitting down. If you sit to watch the game, then it will be harder for other people to pick out who is yelling. Now that you have your spot picked out, it's time to get into the game-play.

As soon as the warmies start, you have to be ready to go. You are watching both teams to see how they look—but most importantly, make sure your kid looks their best. If they aren't skating as hard as they should, start yelling to pick it up. Make sure they are shooting high, too—the biscuits should be hitting c-bar or glass.

As the game starts, it's your time to shine for the next 60 minutes. Anything that the zebras are calling, you should have something to say about. Your kid gets a penalty—you better believe that you are arguing it, trying to get them to reverse the call. If the stripes missed a call, bring out the chirps. Let them know how bad they are and that they are only reffing because they were never any good at playing. To be a great hockey dad, you have to be the loudest in the rink and know the most about the sport.

Always support your kid. Make sure they know that they are the best player on their team and in the league. If they are going to be successful, they need to know that they are the best, and that comes from you. Pump their tires non-stop. Don't put them down if they make a mistake. Instead, teach them to pass the blame onto a teammate (the only kind of passing you should approve of).

It will help them bounce back and probably result in them learning to hold on to the puck longer and mastering the game by themselves. The more your kid has the puck, the more the scouties will take notice, and the better their chances are of getting to the next level.

12 KEY EPPIES

2V2

For many, the Jamie Benn and Tyler Seguin 2v2 eppie stands out as a favourite. We received a lot of feedback about this eppie. We like it, too, but for different reasons. Benn and Seguin took the game, but when you watch it closely, you can see more of our strategy at play. We were in Connecticut at the time for NHL media day and running through the fundies with as many players as possible. It was our job to slingshot players into an even better season, and get the league looking the way we want it to, skill-wise.

The 2v2 is a great test of what players can do. It allowed us to discover areas where these guys needed work. When you look back through the eppie, the first thing that stands out is Benn's hippie on Jacob. Everyone knows hippies are free and served fresh. The hippie technique used was horribly wrong. Jacob's burnin' hoof down the wall, making himself the perfect target for a full-bend hippie. Benn backs in for it but doesn't bend his knees, and with how wobbly they are it should be easy to get nice and low. The lack of knee bend made it nearly impossible for Benn to send Jacob for a full flip to the bone yard. Looking back on the game footy, this is the first thing that stands out. Hippies are key to a successful ice burner. If you can't hit, then you should be a tendy.

Now for Segs. It's plain as paper that he needs *a lot* of help when it comes to hitting. Each and every time he goes near Olly, you can see him toss out the parachute and slow down before heading in. You can't do that, kid. Bury your melon and hit 'em like a Mack Truck. If you want to own the rink, you have to send a message and set the tone before someone else does it for you. As for shooting—what kind of half clapper, almost greasy snapper, hybrid wrist shot was that to "win" the game? Watch that clip again, and listen. That's the sound of a bar-out ball. It's different from the sound of a bar-in ball, and even a back-bar ball. We knew that instantly, but again this 2v2 was to scope out where they need the work.

Understanding the sounds of pipe music is a super-crucie quintessential of the game, and it's clear they don't know how to distinguish the different bass tones of the pipe. We gave them the W with that shot because we couldn't crush their confidence going into the season. Plus, when we get to actually run through the fundies with them again, they won't know what hit 'em!

Another thing to point out about the Benn and Seguin eppie is the way they were laughing the whole time. It's clear they weren't taking it seriously. The fundies aren't a joke, boys. We didn't ask you to come to the blue top. You specifically asked if you could learn from us. Sure, every other coach you have ever had or will ever have won't be nearly as knowledgeable as us, which makes it okay to laugh at the notion that they believe they are teaching you something. But we are the best. You guys are okay, but your tires get pumped too easily by radio and TV talking heads who think they know the game, when in fact they struggle with checkers. Stop listening to them and start focusing, boys!

The whole game plan of the eppie was to let them win. We played the game at 25 percent effort, but made them feel like it was hard on us. This helped expose all their weaknesses in one quick eppie, so we could help them reach the max level of their game. All things considered, they are vets in the league. We don't know how many years we have to get them into top form, and taking it one fundy at a time didn't make sense. We wisely decided to combine all the required fundies into one session and to work fast, so the boys would have an opportunity to utilize the lessons throughout their careers. You're welcome.

THE L.A. DUSTERS

One of the first teams to reach out for some help was the Kings. When we got the call, it was a no brainer to head down to L.A. and see if we could make a difference. This was the first test of the fundies. L.A. isn't the biggest hockey community, so if we were able to make an impact, it would really show the world what we could do.

Immediately, we knew the boys were definitely intimidated by our stature. As they walked onto the

ball hockey rink, you could see the fear in their eyes. This didn't faze us, though. We are pros and know how to get people motivated. We started off slow and took Toff (Tyler Toffoli) under our wing. The kid was in dire need of a better shot. Check back in the eppie and notice how he chokes with someone standing in front and cranks Jacob in the wind box when he shoots. It took a lot of work and countless attempts to finally get him to rip one top corns. With the right advice and superior coaching techniques, we had him ripping any corner at will. It was like a proud father moment seeing him tickle twine at the end of the training.

Jeff Carter was more of a chally. As a vet in the league, he thought he already knew everything about hockey. Getting players like this to commit to the fundies is a hard task. The one thing that we noticed in Jeff's game was how he cellied after a beauty snizz. He was always so plain and his body language was lacklustre. It was the perfect time to start adding some spirit to his celly. He opened up to us quickly and tried firing a harpoon—he almost put the twig straight through Olly's dome. It was a perfect celly as far as we were concerned. To be honest, any celly aside from a little fist pump would have been great to see from this guy.

We know most of you have seen the eppie, so you will remember his attempt at the punt celly. This was when we knew he was trying to be the dominant force on the rink. Olly took that blind side kick straight to the ribs. Jeff claimed sweat had rolled into his eyes, but that was impossible. He just came out from his private little air conditioned tent and cranked Olly. That wasn't a problem, though, we weren't going to give him the reaction he wanted. It's like they say, "If you don't get up, somebody is going to get you up."

Jacob was up next. After the punt incident, we had talked about putting Jeff in his place. Showing off a flag pole celly nose-to-nose with Carter was the perfect remedy for the attitude. When Jacob got elevated to show him what's up, Carter instantly chopped out the twig like a lumberjack. It was at least an eight foot drop straight to the ground. That was the last straw and where the day really seemed to take a turn. Olly came running in—we still don't know why because there was no way he was going to fight anyone, and if he'd known that Kyle Clifford just showed up there's absolutely no way that Olly would have even moved. Clifford's role is to protect his teammates. You can tell just looking at this guy that he isn't getting paid to score all kinds of goals (great guy, though, and if you read this, please don't beat us up). That was the first blood drawn on Olly.

So how do you teach a guy the fundies who just tried to choke you out? We thought about it for around three seconds and it was a no-brainer: let's teach him how to hit. If we get him in the corner, we can run him over and put him back in his place. There was no room to hold a grudge against Cliff, though. We came out to teach, so that's what we were going to do. This guy is a natural-born bruiser, but his meat tossing was average on his best day. Watching the eppie, you will see Olly trying to teach a hippie. It should have been a simple hit to show the kid. Those guys have cheese knees that always wobble, so Clifford should have been able to get nice and low. But Clifford just rolls right through him.

It was vicious, but it was Jacob's turn and there's no room for fear in puck. Since dropping shouldies seemed to be more Clifford's style, we wanted to see how well he could run numbies. The next hit was absolutely textbook. As the bisccy went into the corner, Clifford bowled Jacob over numbies first. Of the three players, Clifford seemed to benefit the most. The kid is tenacious and thanks to us will have a long career in the NHL.

JOHNNY HOCKEY

Want to talk about what the fundies can do for a player who takes them seriously? Johnny Gaudreau is a repeat fundies alumni. The first thing that we need to point out before discussing anything is that when we worked with Johnny the

first time in Boston, we said at the end of the eppie that he would finish the upcoming season with around 86 points. At the end of the season in 2018, Johnny had 85 points. Think that was a coincidence? Absolutely not. We taught him exactly what he needed to know and then told him what he could do with that training. If you listen to our advice and take the fundies seriously, then you will set yourself up for success, just like Johnny Hockey did.

When we met Johnny for the first time, he seemed like a shy, polite young guy that didn't want to offend anyone. You could tell right away, though, that he took hockey very seriously. We met down at the ice to get started. It didn't take a geologist to see that he could barely shoot. It was our job to change that.

We started with his snapper. It only took five rips to see that there was no hope. Olly told him to bury his melon and rip 'em top corns. Johnny steps up and snipes every single shot exactly where he looks. Cool, you can aim. That's the easiest thing to do. But as soon as you aim your shot, it gives the tendy the upper hand because he can see where you are going to shoot. If you don't know where the biscuit is going then no one else knows where it's going either. If you bury your melon and stare at the puck, you'll have the tendy dropping nuggies in his huggies, instantly.

After a brief argument about his snapper, we decided to try out his clapper. Those little chicken wings had a hard time flexing his twig. After he saw Jacob's powerful round-the-world goalie killer clapper, we knew he was impressed and nervous.

That's what it took to get him looking down. He beamed four top corns rippers and sent one pipe music bar out. It was beautiful to see. The kid was getting it and his attitude was changing!

To make it a little more challenging, we wanted to see if he could send a clapper into an empty net from centre ice. We didn't know if he could even shoot a puck that far, let alone hit the net. His eyes went down as he wound up for a clapper and just like we told him it would, the bisccy soared into the net. He didn't even thank us. Actually, he sent one of our twigs to the moon at the end of it all. But that's not why we do what we do. We told him what would happen if he followed the fundies and the amount of points he would be able to put up. At the end of the season, he tallied one less than we said he would get. As pros, that's all the thank you we need.

THE MACDADDY

Some of you don't realize that we don't stop at hockey players. When a living legend like Ron MacLean asks to learn a few things, you step up and take him under your chicken wings. Everyone

who knows anything about puck knows Ron. He is the original MacDaddy, Mr. Mac and Cheese.

When we first met him, we were a little concerned. Ron showed up to our local rink in a fifth line jersey. It took a little bit to help him understand that we don't help refs. This was one of the most difficult people to help because he needed work on everything. Since he doesn't play very much anymore, trying to teach him everything in one fundies session was hard.

We started with some simple passing and discovered that isn't his strong suit. We got up to saucer passes and he almost buckled our knees. We tried to explain to him that a sauce pass is just nice and feathery in the air and lands just in front of the target's twig. Ron must have thought we meant he should send heat seekers at our knee caps. In the end we agreed that he would keep the biscuit on the ice in order to ensure the safety of his teammates.

Next we worked on a few shots. You can't expect a desk jockey to send laser beams. Naturally, just like everything else, we were right. Ron did have one thing down pat, though: on every shot he had his melon buried and no one in that rink had any idea where those shots were going. We left him with some homework to fire between 50 and 3,000 shots a day to work on the power of his snapper.

Since he sits behind a desk, we thought for some final fundies we would work on something he could take back to the office. Hopping the boards on a line change may be one of the most overlooked fundies. The reason we chose this is because if he ever needs a quick out when Grapes is giving him a bad time, he could just quickly hop and split the set. Board hops are easy for us and you can see the elevation from our ridiculous vertical jumps when we're getting on the ice. It turned out that Ron is more of a gate guy, making sure his teammate has an easy-off and can come out with speed into the play.

All jokes aside, it was an honour to work with Ron MacDaddy. Growing up watching *Hockey Night in Canada* and listening to Ron and Don talk about everything hockey was probably every Canadian's Saturday night. These guys were the definition of hockey until we came into the game, but they have stayed a close second to us. One day it's going to be Olly and Jacob ripping up the desk. Just let us know when you are ready to retire, boys, and we will do you proud filling your shoes!

VEGAS: THE COVER SCANDAL

This isn't really a fundy, but we thought we should take a minute and talk about what happened to us in Vegas. Getting that call to head to the NHL Awards was a dream come true. We could have, and probably should have, scooped up all those awards. It's easy to see that we snizz the best, going top corns every morns. And you bet we are a shoo-in for the Byng, two of the biggest beauties and gentlemen in the game. That's not what we went for, though—awards have always been an easy targgy for us. That cover spot on EA Sports' *NHL 19* was what we were looking for and honestly should have had.

We flew in on the red eye—it was like 10:00 in the morning when we left Cow-town—and were eager to get on that stage and walk right onto the cover of chel. In Sin City we hit Ross, the classiest store to get fresh gear from, and prepped our acceptance

speeches. We barely slept more than 12 hours that night, we were so stoked.

Then it all went wrong. We got called to the staging area and were told we'd be going on in five minutes. It's a live show, so we had to read a prompter. It was all good, though—we are basically made of steel, purebred machines, and nothing fazes us. We hit the stage, following the instructions and script on the teleprompter, and everyone knows what happened next. The cover got tossed to P.K. Subban. Not that he doesn't deserve it—he's a great guy and a great player. But come on! With chel adding in the new O.D.R. mode—that's where we created, mastered, and absolutely dommed the fundies! There's no question that chel cover belongs to us. We were a little rattled with the rundown, but we don't let things bug us for more than a few months.

13 LEGENDS LOUNGE: INTERVIEWS AND Q&Q

RON "MACDADDY" MACLEAN

Original GOAT: Greatest Of All Time. That's the easiest way to describe this beauty. Ron MacLean single-handedly put Red Deer, Alberta, on the map and is a household name across all of Canada. He's a first line to fifth line kind of guy. That means twisting twig and burning biscuits, as well as rocking the zebra print and orange tattoo. Almost like a loose cannon, you never know whose side he's on.

MacLean hasn't always been a fan of a good celly, but that all changed when he learned some fundies from us. We turned him on to the idea, and we are pretty sure he wants to see more of it in the game now. Ron is an honoured member of the Fundies Alumni and one of the first to master the skills. It's also rumoured that he wants to commit more time with us to hone new skills. (His clapper is a long way from making tendies drop nuggies in their huggies.) We had a chance to spend time with the GOAT and ask a few quesys. Here's what he had to say.

OTB: Did it take you so long to reach out for fundies because you were afraid of us?

MACLEAN: My fear of you two came down to the fact we'd be filming *On the Bench*. I was horrible at spitting and no self-respecting pro is a poor spitter. I felt I'd be getting a little ahead of myself if I came without spit. You saliva devils are intimidating. It was only when you said, "Just bring a crispy rhyme" that I stood tall. Turns out you're two of the nicest guys I've come across.

OTB: How come you haven't asked us to spare for your men's league team?

MACLEAN: Well, that's an easy one. My team can't spit and don't celly. Now that you've taught me to celly, the three of us together would be like tripling myself. Messy.

OTB: Do you think our fundies have made an impact on the NHL?

MACLEAN: *On the Bench* fundies are the reason there are more pucks flying over the glass than ever before. Fans are so excited, they're screaming, dancing, bleeding in their seats. But ya gotta be up for it—you show up on date night and it's rubber everywhere.

OTB: Of all the players in the game, who needs our coaching the most?

MACLEAN: That's Alex Ovechkin. You see all the carrying on after the Cup. Keg stands, swimming in public fountains, partying all over the world. No way you guys would have done that. You would have been far worse.

OTB: What made you like cellys so much?

MACLEAN: I like cellys because they remind me of cellophane. Invisible but effective at preserving the good stuff. It's weird but I grew up with the Lanny McDonald "Mr. Wrap-Around," and so I connect him with celly swagger. When we were all together in Canmore, Lanny convinced me to celly my soul.

OTB: When can we expect to be a part of *Coach's Corner*? Considering we are the best coaches and there's room for four.

MACLEAN: I'd love to give you the green light and have you join us in The Corner. The more "buds," the merrier. But you keep giving us the red lights . . .

JACKIE REDMOND

If you watch any sort of sports highlights, you know the name Jackie Redmond. She is easily one of if not the highest-ranking legends when it comes to sports highlights and interviews. Our best interviews are easily the ones we have done with her. She always asks the hard-hitting quesys and isn't afraid to stir the pot. If we weren't in queue to take over *Coach's Corner*, Jackie for sure would scoop the position. Oh, and you can't forget the fact that she is a Canadian girl, which means she was born a natural at everything.

OTB: Out of the three of us, who has the best hair? You, Olly, or Jacob?

REDMOND: Well, I'll refrain from choosing myself since having extensions likely disqualifies me from the competition. I'm going to go with Jacob simply because his blond locks tend to flip outward away from the face much like Farrah Fawcett in *Charlie's Angels*, and if that doesn't cause hair envy in 90 percent of women, I don't know what does.

OTB: Do you laugh so much during our interviews because you are nervous?

REDMOND: It's probably 50 percent because I'm trying to get the attention back on me and 50 percent because of my *Tiger Beat* crushie on Jacob.

OTB: Out of all the fundies, which help you the most at work?

REDMOND: I'm going to go with the episode on getting respect in the new dressing room that featured Jordan Eberle. As you know, I joined the NHL Network in free agency and wanted to make a good first impression. So, I showed up day one and demanded the best office, stole the best desk chair from an NHL Network vettie, and "accidentally" knocked Jamie Hersch's wardrobe rack onto the floor. Nobody messes with me now, and it's all thanks to you guys and your fundies!

OTB: Which co-host would you like to hippie the most?

REDMOND: Barry Melrose. Melly's been around forever. If I hippie him, everyone will *have* to respect me, right?

OTB: Who is your favourite hockey team?

REDMOND: The Toronto Maple Leafs. They're a Cup contendy this year. It's not a big deal.

OTB: Is it true you want to challenge us to see who can hit all three posts first?

REDMOND: 100 percent. I hit three targets last year while blindfolded. I ain't scared. Plus, I've been waiting to debut a new celly—so bring it on, boys!

OTB: When do you want to learn some fundies in an eppie?

REDMOND: Like, yesterday.

OTB: Why did you want to interview us so badly?

REDMOND: Obvi, to try to poach some of your followers.

BROCK BOESER

Who doesn't like broccoli? Although a young gun, he stamped his career and status as a legend when he came into the league. A future Hall of Famer, for sure. This kid has just about everything you need in a hockey player. From his deadly lettuce, to his soft hands rippin' snappers and breaking defencemen's ankles, all the way to his hockey sense—this kid is a natural shoo-in for the Legends Lounge. The only thing we would like him to improve on is the amount of penalties he takes—you have to ramp that up, kid! And, of course, some scrapping. We're pretty sure he hasn't been in a tilly before. We can't be upset, though; he's been calling us weekly to get a first-hand fundies tutorial. When he's ready, we will take him to the next level!

OTB: Is it true you gave yourself the nickname "Prince Charming"?

BOESER: Yeah, it's true I gave myself the nickname. I mean, come on, have you not seen the movie? I look identical to the guy.

OTB: Of all the players in the league, who would you beat in a scrap?

BOESER: No career fights under my belt yet, so probably Anders Bjork because he's my buddy and thinks he's tough.

OTB: Do you think you're ready for some fundies and some actual good coaching from us?

BOESER: I definitely need the coaching. I think I need some more grit to my game and a coach to teach me how to check the right way and not get hurt.

OTB: Who's better, you or Nathan MacKinnon? Be honest, no modesty.

BOESER: Let's be real: MacKinnon. The guy is lightning fast.

OTB: What's your favourite celly?

BOESER: Not a big celly guy, but usually putting the sword away.

OTB: Why don't you use our cellys when you rip rope?

BOESER: I don't use your cellys because I need a live demo.

OTB: What superpower would you want to have and why?

BOESER: To fly and float in the sky.

OTB: Is it true you wanted to be in Herbal Essences commercials as a kid?

BOESER: Maybe it's true. I mean, I feel my parents gave me good enough hair growing up to star in a commercial.

OTB: How do we get a T-shirt like the one with your face all over it?

BOESER: Search "the flow Boeser T-shirt" on the Web and click "order."

OTB: Which fundies do you need the most work on?

BOESER: Toughen me up.

BRETT KISSEL

To have any sort of success when you're playing puck, you need to get pumped up. Every game is a big game because you never know how many scouties are going to be in the stands. You need to be ready to go. Even if there aren't any at that game, you can guarantee that the rocket recliners are going to be full. Music is the easiest way to get fired up pre-game. Having one of Canada's best pumping through the speakers is a no-brainer.

Brett Kissel took some advice from us on his historic "We Were That Song" tour to get the crowd fired up. Apparently, it was the most extensive tour

in Canadian music—and it's probably safe to say that using some of our fundies helped this guy get the most nominations at the Canadian Country Music Awards, with a cool six nods. The kid also won Male Artist of the Year, got a big plaque or something from Canada's Walk of Fame, and even won a Juno Award, all by following our recipe for success.

Brett is a good ol' Alberta boy, purebred beauty, and proud member of the Fundies Alumni, so it's a no-brainer to have him in the Legends Lounge. We asked him how working with Olly and Jacob helped his music game.

OTB: How did the fundies help you on tour?

KISSEL: I realized I was doing it all wrong before I met the boys. I thought I was decent at firing up a crowd, but I am now aware of what it takes in terms of energy, showmanship, and sex appeal to really get the crowd going for a big show!

OTB: When are you going to grow out the lettuce?

KISSEL: When I was a kid, I had a mullet that had no rival—except maybe Jaromir Jagr. In the next few years, I'm seriously considering getting my greasy flow back, and letting those piles of curls just melt the fans from under my cowboy hat.

OTB: Why don't you have a stampede strap on your hat, like Jacob does?

KISSEL: I don't know actually. I'm gonna call the Calgary Stampede and ask what Jacob has that I don't have.

OTB: Is it true "We Were That Song" was written about our friendship?

KISSEL: No. Not at all.

OTB: If you could pick any two players to make a line with, who would you pick?

KISSEL: Connor McDavid would be my C. Jordan Eberle would be my RW. I'd be on the LW tappin' in some juicy rebounds.

OTB: Who do you think would crush a national anthem, Olly or Jacob?

KISSEL: Neither. The anthem singer is the riskiest position to play out there on the ice. If you nail it, people cheer, but it gets very little attention. If you mess it up, people boo and you're a YouTube failure forever.

OTB: Are you almost ready to get some fundies on how to soothe a mic?

KISSEL: What does that even mean?

OTB: Are we still on board to write and sing the next hockey anthem?

KISSEL: I think the NHL is due for the next big hockey song. I wrote one during the last lockout, but we could write something pretty great, I am certain of it.

TEDDY PURCELL

This guy defines legend. If you haven't heard of him, then you don't even know hockey, and how can you even call yourself a fan? This purebred from St. John's tore up the league and was brought to Tampa Bay to help some other legends like Vinny Lecavalier and Steven Stamkos rip more rope. One thing that most people don't know about Teddy is that he's bilingual—speaking English and Newfoundlander!

OTB: What was your favourite club to play for?

PURCELL: My favourite team I played for was Tampa Bay. I also loved playing in L.A., and it's where I live now, but I really became a full-time NHL player in Tampa. I was a pigeon when I first

started in L.A. The coach was a fossil and hated me and most young guys, besides [Drew] Doughty. We weren't all as good as Dewy, so I was told to ship it to Tampa. I was lucky I got to play with so many good players. Passing to Marty [Martin St. Louis] and Vinny and Stammer made me look good, so I can thank them for the six years of contracts I got from the Lightning.

OTB: Of all the guys in the league, who is the one you want to serve a folded five to?

PURCELL: Haha! Well, if I was tough, I would've handed them out a lot without thinking of sh**ting in my diaper when it was their turn to punch me back. Tampa and Boston were in the same division, so we played them a lot in the regular season and then had a fun Eastern Conference final against them. Initially, I hated [Brad] Marchand—thought he was cocky and annoying. And also the fact that he could smoke a cigarette in the shower with that nose he has. So probably him at the time. But I was in Boston training camp last year and got to know him and watch him go to work every day. I was so impressed by his drive and how competitive he is. Everyone knows how good and skilled he is. He's also a good dude. Funny how those things usually end up that way in hockey.

OTB: Who invented the Larryashy?

PURCELL: The Larryashy was created by a couple Belleville boys: Brad Richardson and his best buddy, Kyle Reid. They both taught me a lot about how to keep their ash the longest on their ciggy while smoking it. After 12 beers, and once we mastered the trick, we would then say what kind of curve was on the ashy. I always went with the [Chris] Drury pattern. Richy was more of a [Joe] Sakic kinda guy.

OTB: Is it true playing in Edmonton was your biggest regret in life?

PURCELL: Edmonton. Ugh. I don't regret it because I was traded there, so I had no choice. But it's not a coincidence most free agents don't sign there. The guys were great, but that's all we had. Going out for a bite to eat or a beer and having these "heroes" saying we suck and are overpaid and we don't deserve to have fun was painful. The town is so ugly, too. But one day I can tell my kids I taught 97 [Connor McDavid] how to dress like a human and how to talk to a girl.

OTB: Least favourite coach and why?

PURCELL: Most coaches I had wanted to choke me out. I don't blame 'em. But one assistant stands out: Davis Payne. What a nerd this guy was, and I only had him for a few months. Complete hardo, acted like he played 1,500 NHL games. Acted like he was tougher than Bob Probert, and more skilled than Brett Hull. He asked me to "try him" on the bench one game when we were beating Calgary 4–1 or something. After the game I'm like, I gotta look this guy up. He's such a bluff. Played 22 NHL games, had one assist. Wasn't even a point-per-game guy in the ECHL. And he would walk around all day, mean mugging, and the grumpiest person in the NHL I've ever seen.

OTB: Who do you like better, Jacob or Olly?

PURCELL: Jacob or Olly? I hate both of you. But thanks for including me in the Legends Lounge. I consider this my Hall of Fame off-the-ice moment.

LEGENDS IN THE MODERN GAME OF PUCK (BESIDES POSTANIN AND ARDOWN)

1. *The Big E,* Eric Lindros
2. *Mr. Lip Sweater,* Lanny McDonald
3. *Kid Clapper,* Al MacInnis
4. *Blue Line Bomber,* Al Iafrate
5. *Liquid Fireman,* Tim Horton
6. *Mr. Opinion,* Don "Grapes" Cherry
7. *The MacDaddy,* Ron MacLean
8. *Self-Proclaimed Prince Charming,* Brock Boeser
9. *Johnny Hockey,* Johnny Gaudreau

10. ***The Real Deal,*** James Neal
11. ***Dot Destroyer,*** Mark Scheifele
12. ***Captain Humble,*** Connor McDavid
13. ***The Mighty Mite,*** Jason Zucker
14. ***The Pillow Piler,*** Marc-André Fleury
15. ***The Cheese Wheel,*** Radko Gudas

CONCLUSION: FUNDIES FOR LIFE!

Fundies aren't just for hockey. Apply what you've learned here to everyday life. Be super greasy. Respect the flow. Whatever you do and wherever you are, be the cappy on any and every team. In life, always shoot top corns, and remember to celly hard, kid. You've earned it.

HEAVEN'S
FIRST LINE

TRIBUTE TO HUMBOLDT

The hockey community is worldwide, and a lot closer than you may think. Unfortunately, it often takes something tragic to remind us of that. On April 6, 2018, the Humboldt Broncos were in a tragic accident on their way to a playoff game. We all know the story of what happened, as it was covered in all areas of the news and social media. This is just a small reminder to enjoy the good things in life, like the bus trips, the stories, and all the laughs. Hockey creates a family, not just a team but a family. For anyone who hasn't ever played on a team before, it's difficult to fully explain. When we say hockey isn't just a game, there's a reason for that. We want to pay our respects to all the athletes, families, and friends that were shaken by this tragedy. Our thoughts and prayers will always remain with you, and we know that every game we play, heaven's first line is watching over us! #HumboldtStrong

ACKNOWLEDGEMENTS

To all our fans out there. Thank you for following us, interacting with us, and helping us teach the fundies. Without you watching, sharing, liking, and following, we wouldn't be in these cowboy boots and Velcro runners, helping everything in hockey get better, and remembering to laugh and enjoy it every single day. We couldn't do what we do without you!

A very special thank you to those who helped produce this amazing piece of nonfiction—while we did most of the work, we know these folks spent a few minutes helping it come together. Our Manager DaleAnn Murphy for everything she does for us—she's the MVP of our first ever written eppie; our Literary Agent Brian Wood for landing us this sweet off-ice conny; our Editors Justin Stoller and Alanna McMullen for helping grease through the process; Publisher of Penguin Canada Nicole Winstanley for championing us; Andrew Roberts for designing this beauty of a book; Managing Editor David Ross, Production Editor Kate Panek,

Copy Editor Valerie Adams, Proofreader Crissy Calhoun, and Typesetter Sean Tai all deserve apples for being deadly teamies; and our Publicist Ruta Liormonas for hitting top corns on getting this book to the benders who really need it and scoring us all sorts of innies.

NOTE FROM STEVEN CAMPBELL (OLLY)

Before we take off, boys, I want to say thank you to all of you beauties for watching our videos, liking our content, and following us for so long. We wouldn't be doing these videos without you. To all the players over the past year who jumped on to film with us, and to all the fans who showed up to our meet-and-greets, you're all legends. Also to D, our manager, for the countless hours and hard work—without you, we wouldn't be where we are today. To the brands that have believed in us, the NHL teams who posted our content, and to the league itself for making our dreams come true, we can't thank you guys enough.

NOTE FROM RYAN RUSSELL (JACOB)

The concept of *On the Bench* came from the desire to bring out the fun in hockey and add more enjoyment to the game. We created the fundies to help kids stay in the game and develop a continuing passion for hockey.

We have been fortunate, to say the least, throughout this insane roller-coaster ride as Olly and Jacob. It is an absolute honour to have the opportunity to meet and work with the real greats of the game. But making people smile and laugh takes the cake. Our goal was to make a positive difference in people's lives and I believe we do. That's all thanks to every single one of you that watches, shares, likes, and gives us feedback. Be it positive or negative feedback, it all helps move us forward. We keep listening, so *On the Bench* can continue to make you laugh and enjoy the game.

Personally, hockey has always been a huge part of my life and it always will be. My hope is to share my passion with the world in a way that gets more people playing the game I love, and inspire those who may have lost that love to regain it. If nothing else, I hope that we have been successful in making you smile and maybe even helped make a hard day a little easier to get through.

Thank you everyone for reading this book and supporting us. We wouldn't be in our position if it weren't for everyone helping us get there.